Praise for *Extraterrestrial Contact*

"Finally, there is a (much-needed and long-awaited) practical handbook for anyone looking for guidance on how to comprehend, evaluate, and digest alien abduction memories into the framework of life in the 21st century . . . an eye-opening bridge for future generations, as it is predicted humanity will likely inhabit another planet by the end of the next century. If contact is inevitable, perhaps those who have been abducted will one day be honored as our evolutionary ambassadors."

—Jennifer W. Stein, documentary producer for
Travis: The True Story of Travis Walton

"Once again, author and investigator Kathleen Marden has made a remarkable contribution to the world of serious UFO literature. This wealth of practical, well-documented information contained in *Extraterrestrial Contact: What to Do When You've Been Abducted* will be invaluable to experiencers and abductees as well as to educators, mental health professionals, and serious students of ufology worldwide."

—Peter Robbins, author, investigative writer,
and long-time assistant to pioneer
UFO abduction researcher Budd Hopkins

"A book long overdue that will undoubtedly be an instrumental go-to manual for anyone haunted by their recurring dreams and half memories. A beacon for the lost in need of solace and a reassurance they are not alone.

"There can never be enough praise for Kathleen Marden and her work, which will bring us closer to unraveling the abduction mystery and empower people from all walks of life to shine the light on this reality."

—Yvonne Smith, CHT, author of *Chosen* and *Coronado*

"Kathleen Marden continues to be a leader in the search into the mystifying saga of paranormal contact. She is a notable presenter on the phenomena, and her groundbreaking work cannot be ignored. I admire Kathleen as well as Anne Castle, Denise Stoner, and Mady Tobias—brave women, who are clear-headed, compassionate investigators."

—Derrel Sims, RHA, CMHt, The Alien Hunter

EXTRA TERRESTRIAL CONTACT

EXTRA TERRESTRIAL CONTACT

what to do when you've been ABDUCTED

KATHLEEN MARDEN

MUFON
Mutual UFO Network
— est. 1969 —

This edition first published in 2019 by MUFON an imprint of
Red Wheel/Weiser, LLC
With offices at:
65 Parker Street, Suite 7
Newburyport, MA 01950
www.redwheelweiser.com

ISBN: 978-1-59003-301-2
Library of Congress Cataloging-in-Publication Data available upon request.

Cover design by Kathryn Sky-Peck
Cover photograph by Shutterstock
Interior by Timm Bryson, em em design, LLC
Typeset in Minion Pro

Printed in the United States of America
LB
10 9 8 7 6 5 4 3 2 1

*I would like to dedicate this book to the brave pioneers
who paved the way to better understanding
of the ET contact phenomenon:*

*Dr. James Harder, Coral Lorenzen, Dr. Leo Sprinkle,
Barbara Lamb, Ann Druffel, Budd Hopkins,
Dr. David Jacobs, Betty Hill, Dr. Thomas Bullard,
Raymond Fowler, and Yvonne Smith.*

Contents

Acknowledgments

I would like to acknowledge the hard-working, compassionate volunteers on MUFON's Experiencer Research Team, who volunteer their time to help experiencers.

EXTRA
TERRESTRIAL
CONTACT

Introduction

Twenty years have passed since Ann Druffel, a prominent UFO researcher, wrote her seminal book *How to Defend Yourself Against Alien Abduction.*[1] Her daughter accepted a lifetime achievement award on her behalf at the 2018 International UFO Congress Conference near Phoenix, Arizona. Ann's research led her to conclude that our extraterrestrial visitors are, in fact, negative interdimensional entities whose invasive, harassing agenda fuels their penchant for feeding off human fear and suffering. In her effort to help her fellow humans, she collected documented evidence that indicates some people had successfully fended off attacks by the abducting Grey entities, long thought to be of extraterrestrial origin. The nine techniques that abductees believed were successful are outlined in her book. I recommend it to experiencers who write to me seeking help with this problem, but I know of no comprehensive, updated guide for experiencers in general.

Our knowledge and understanding of contact with nonhuman intelligence or nonhuman intelligent (NHI) entities has increased exponentially over the past twenty years, as researchers, including myself, have gained additional knowledge pertaining to the NHI entities who have inserted themselves into the lives of thousands, if not millions of Earthlings from around our planet. Contact transcends race, religion, social class, educational level, cultural ethos, values, beliefs, and the state of one's mental health. It affects a multitude of

Earthlings at many levels. Some contact is decidedly positive and highly spiritual, whereas some is terrifyingly negative, even evil. It runs the gamut, crossing many lines and belief systems. It is extraordinary and unsettling. It is the greatest mystery of our time.

In 2011, the Mutual UFO Network (MUFON), an organization of which I have been a member since 1991, appointed me Director of Abduction Research. Despite the protestations of some MUFON members, I worked with a multidisciplinary team of consultants to establish protocols for the investigation of alien abductions. I had read a series of complaints on social media sites that concerned me. The grumblers stated that they had gone to MUFON seeking help with their experiences but had not received it. I had to identify the problem. What kind of help had they sought? Was it help that MUFON offered? Many people thought, erroneously, that MUFON had federal funding to offer medical treatment and hypnotherapy to abductees. Their expectations were not founded in reality, and there were no clear guidelines to set them straight. This is one of the first problems I tackled. I also set up a program to offer nonjudgmental listening to abductees because most people were looking for some kind of assistance. At first, I was the only Experiencer Research Team (ERT) member that spoke with people seeking help. But the job soon outgrew my free time.

Over the next several years, I expanded MUFON's Abduction Research Team and altered its title to Experiencer Research Team, because not all contact events are abductions. The ERT now has eighteen supportive members, who engage in nonjudgmental listening with individuals that have completed the Experiencer Questionnaire on MUFON's website. Most experiencers would agree that the simple act of discussing their troubling suspicions and doubts, confidentially and without criticism, has offered both comfort and a sense of liberation to them. MUFON's ERT performs much like a triage team, to assist experiencers in identifying their personal needs. Team members maintain a list of vetted licensed professional therapists, certified hypnotists with specialized training, and self-help support groups specifically for experiencers who wish to enter into a private relationship with a therapist or support person beyond the scope of what MUFON offers.

I am grateful to Dr. George Medich, the ERT's assistant director, for his administration of the day-to-day operations, while I work to educate the public and assist experiencers through my books, media appearances, presentations, and hypnosis sessions.

MUFON does not recommend, refer, or endorse any individual or organization on the ERT's list. We encourage experiencers to undertake due diligence with each individual on our list, acknowledging that risks are inherent in using any support provider. MUFON does not provide medical advice or encourage experiencers to seek professional services. Under no circumstances will MUFON be liable for any damages to the user of the directory either direct, indirect, incidental, special, punitive, or consequential that result in any way from an experiencer's use of or inability to use MUFON's informational list. The individuals listed on MUFON's directory are not employed by MUFON. They are in private practice and expect payment for their services.

For years, experiencers have struggled to find answers to their multitude of questions. Many have suffered greatly. While contact with NHI entities was being debated by UFO researchers, skeptics, and academics, experiencers were suffering in silence. The focus was on the veracity of the abductees' claims and the physical evidence. The emotional struggle was often not met with compassion or understanding. Experiencers were accused of being liars, even when they were telling the truth; attention seekers, when they did not seek attention; and mentally ill, even when they were psychologically healthy. Under siege from all sides, experiencers were subjected to feelings of fear and loathing. Even those experiencers who had substantial evidence were mistreated if their information was made public. Humans inflicted intolerable pain upon other humans. The insensitivity of some prominent skeptics was horrendous.

Academic studies sought to identify the reasons why UFO experiencers embraced so-called delusional ideology, when the scientific community "knew" that intragalactic space travel was impossible. Federal agencies had done a marvelous job covering up the facts and feeding the public a false belief system. Experts were hauled in front of the public to reassure the ignorant that sleep paralysis, personality disorders, misperception, and a variety of other explanations could explain all claims of alien abduction. They failed to mention that these common explanations did not pertain to most experiencers.

Abductees insisted that they had been removed from their natural environment and transported by NHI entities to an unfamiliar setting that was both alien and unearthly. Many had conscious recall of observing silent, hovering craft, in close proximity to their location, prior to their transfer to an alien environment. They had observed NHI entities in close proximity to or aboard unconventional craft far in advance of our technological development. Most abductees who completed a battery of psychological tests were deemed normal. However, there was a slightly elevated level of fantasy proneness and personality disorders among some. Psychologists identified an increased level of trauma among abductees, as if they had been subjected to a real traumatic event. (We explore this issue in Chapter 4.) Even today, many experiencers are apprehensive when it comes to trusting anyone with their secrets. Too many people keep their feelings bottled up inside while they suffer in silence.

The majority of experiencers who remember physical contact (i.e., UFO abductees) are initially terrified by troubling memories and increased anxiety related to their experiences. These include loss of control, fear of the unknown, the possibility that they won't be returned to their natural environment, fear of being harmed, and fear of the NHI entities' physical appearance.

The majority of experiencers have prefaced their remarks to me with "I know that this sounds crazy." My greatest concern lies in the fact that experiencers of contact with NHI entities feel they must apologize or write self-effacing remarks in their opening statements to me. Some wish they could receive a diagnosis for a major mental illness because mental illness can be treated and their living hell will finally end. Others have become accustomed to abduction and, after many years, have moved beyond fear toward friendly, egalitarian contact.

I have investigated reports of contact with NHI entities since 1988 and have had a personal interest in alien abduction for more than fifty-eight years. I witnessed the emotional impact that contact had on my aunt and uncle, Betty and Barney Hill, and the toll it took on them when disinformants sought to discredit them and their documented experience. (For a comprehensive case study of the Hill case, see my book with Stanton Friedman, *Captured! The Betty and Barney Hill UFO Experience,* 2007.)

My own memories of contact and the nocturnal terror they caused have led to years of research for conclusive answers regarding the reality of contact and how to live comfortably as an experiencer. I have developed a proactive approach to the many complex components of contact and have identified the differences between contact with benevolent spiritual entities, contact with a variety of NHI entities who might be extraterrestrial entities, and harassment by interdimensional entities, parasites, and demons. I have also researched methods that might curtail or end abduction if the experiencer desires it. I think of myself as an experiencer advocate and a proponent of every experiencer's right to be treated with respect and dignity. I share my personal experiences and insights in this handbook, in the hope that they will help everyone who reads it. I also introduce information, sometimes frightening and sometimes heartwarming, that will give you insight into what is really occurring.

In an effort to learn more, I have spearheaded one small and one comprehensive study to identify commonalities among experiencers. In 2012, my investigation partner and coauthor of *The Alien Abduction Files,* Denise Stoner, and I conducted a small but important study that identified twenty-three commonalities among abduction experiencers that are not common in the general population. Next, I participated in developing the Phase 1 Experiencer Questionnaire for the Dr. Edgar Mitchell Foundation for Research Into Extraterrestrial and Extraordinary Encounters (FREE). FREE has completed the first comprehensive investigation on more than three thousand individuals who believe they have had various forms of contact with NHI entities regardless of whether or not a UFO was sighted. Then in 2018, Dr. Don C. Donderi and I completed a major multiyear experiencer research project for MUFON. Our goal was to identify a host of characteristics that experiencers share and to separate the abductees from the contactees among the participants.

I am a member of FREE Board of Directors. FREE is an organization of academics, scientists, and lay researchers dedicated to the study of consciousness. As I stated earlier, not all contact with NHI entities is frightening or negative. The majority of participants in FREE's study believe they have had ongoing contact and communication with highly positive, physical, and nonphysical NHI entities.

Much of my work has been accomplished on a volunteer basis for the benefit of experiencers everywhere. This is more often the rule than the exception among researchers of UFOs and contact, primarily because abduction has been identified as a fringe topic and is considered politically taboo. This is the case despite the work of numerous brave, highly regarded scientists who have deemed it worthy of scientific study, including Dr. J. Allen Hynek, Dr. James E. McDonald, Dr. James Harder, Dr. Robert Wood, Dr. Jacques Vallée, and Stanton T. Friedman, MSc. (A detailed history of this topic is available in *Fact, Fiction, and Flying Saucers* [2016], my latest book with Stanton T. Friedman.)

I feel uniquely qualified to research contact with NHI entities because of my academic background in the social sciences: sociology, psychology, and social work. I participated in graduate studies in education while I was employed as an educator. Additionally, I have performed journalistic research on topics such as hypnosis, sleep paralysis, sleep hallucinations, and personality disorders, and various academic studies on abduction experiencers. To round out my work, I completed an educational program to qualify as a certified hypnotherapist. I also completed advanced training in techniques that can be applied to work successfully with experiencers. I share this information with you in this book. Since my retirement, I have worked as an international speaker, on-camera expert, and author.

I have invited three of my colleagues to contribute their own chapters to this book. Each is a specialist in her field of study. They are Ann Castle, Denise Stoner, and Madeline Tobias.

Ann Castle is a dedicated member of the MUFON Experiencer Research Team who has lent her expertise and intuition in helping experiencers integrate their unique histories into a more meaningful life. Her thirty-year background in psychology, consciousness, the paranormal, and abductions has made her a valuable part of the ERT. Her background in psychology has contributed to her success in helping experiencers in Texas and Florida process and integrate their unique histories into their lives.

Ann has written numerous articles for the *Journal of Abnormal Abduction Research* (*JAAR*) and is active in the Jacksonville ET Abduction/Experiencer Support Group. Ann is a clairvoyant who researches consciousness and the quantum field. She has teamed with law enforcement in four countries and has found dozens of missing persons and other targets.

Her interests in UFOs and missing persons culminated in her novel, *Captured Souls,* which combines facts she encountered in her UFO and missing persons investigations. I think that you will benefit from Ann's expertise and wisdom.

Denise Stoner is Special Assistant to the Directors of MUFON's Experiencers Research Team. She is also involved in Florida MUFON as a State Section Director, Field Investigator, Star Team Member, and former Florida MUFON Chief Investigator.

Her personal history of alien abduction dates back to age two and a half and has continued throughout her lifetime. Hers is one of six major cases I investigated and documented in *The Alien Abduction Files,* a book that Denise and I coauthored. In 2012, she and I conducted a small study on the commonalities that experiencers share. We identified twenty-three commonalities among forty-six choices. Denise has contributed questions to phase 1 of FREE's Experiencer Questionnaire and to MUFON's Experiencer Survey.

Denise holds educational forums for public and private gatherings for abduction experiencers. Her involvement in the UFO field spans more than thirty years. She hosted an Experiencer's Workshop at MUFON's International Symposium in 2016.

Denise has an educational background in business and psychology, and holds an associate's degree in business. She is a certified hypnotist specializing in hypnotic regression. She has taught classes in stress reduction for more than twelve years for professionals in such fields as medicine and law.

She began her research in hypnosis under Dr. Bob Romack (Denver, Colorado). They worked together for five years on pain control, smoking cessation, and past life regression research. Denise also worked as a paranormal investigator in the homes of abductees who felt they had been visited by spirits following abductions. She recorded evidence of the development of psychic abilities in individuals following their experiences with UFOs and ETs, and worked on a team with Dr. Romack studying abductees' abilities to locate missing people and predict future events. Her certification in hypnosis and hypnotic regression came through the Hypnotic Research Society by Dr. Ronald P. De Vasto. Advanced regression study was accomplished through the National Guild of Hypnotists, Inc. by Donald J. Mottin.

Her retirement from the federal government has allowed her to expand her work with UFO research and investigation. Denise has appeared on the Travel Channel, PBS's *Weird Florida* with Charlie Carlson, and more than one hundred radio shows. She has lectured at the Daytona Museum of Arts and Science, Exeter (New Hampshire) UFO Festival, and other venues. She has worked as an on-camera expert for documentaries produced in the UK, Japan, and Italy.

Denise continues to further her education and research and is presently taking a college-level course with Bishop James Long on all things paranormal. The modules also include topics such as angels, demons, and parasites. Bishop Long is presenting this course in order to educate those who work in the field and are interested in an even more solid base of information to help others. He generously donates all fees to his homeless mission.

As a result of Denise's continuous years of "on the ground" research and study in a field that has suddenly found a connection with the UFO/ET field, she addresses and approaches it using her eyes, ears, and education in all of these fields. This knowledge helps those who need support in understanding the variety of these odd events in their lives and where the pieces fit together.

Madeleine (Mady) Tobias is a retired psychotherapist who worked with veterans with post-traumatic stress disorder (PTSD) from combat trauma and sexual abuse. She started private practice in 1981, and is a clinical specialist in Adult Psychiatric and Mental Health Counseling. She holds a master's of science degree in education/counseling.

Mady became a MUFON Field Investigator in 2016 and was immediately drawn to helping experiencers and those affected by their exposure to the UFO phenomena. She has had a lifelong interest in ufology and the paranormal.

She is the author of books and articles on helping those recovering from experiences with mind control in destructive cults. She sees many similarities in the aftereffects of both destructive cults and abduction experiences.

Together we have taken a proactive approach toward finding solutions and offering suggestions that might help experiencers overcome their struggles with shame and victimization. In *Extraterrestrial Contact: What to Do When You've Been Abducted,* we bring our years of knowledge and experience to the table for the benefit of those who are attempting to cope with their memories of contact with NHI entities. We discuss possible alternative explanations and offer practical suggestions on how to develop effective coping skills. If you suspect that you may have been abducted by NHI entities, if you've had friendly contact, if you have not been able to identify precisely what is occurring in your life, and if you are attempting to cope with this possibility, *Extraterrestrial Contact: What to Do When You've Been Abducted* is for you.

Chapter 1

UNDERSTANDING MODERN CONTACT

Kathleen Marden

Dating back to the 1950s, contact with nonhuman intelligent (NHI) entities was highly positive and spiritually enlightening. There was nothing to fear and no one experienced trauma. Contact involved communication with benevolent space brothers and sisters by spiritually enlightened leaders. They brought forth messages that warned us of the destructive nature of nuclear weapons and the importance of being good stewards of our planet.

George Adamski, the most famous contactee of that era, and many others advised their followers that space brothers of human appearance were intermingling with the people of Earth, in an effort to guide us to a state of higher awareness—of spiritual ascension. These benevolent beings promised to share their medical and technological secrets with us as soon as humankind has matured and transformed into one altruistic society. The conditions upon which we would be permitted to tap into this knowledge required environmental respect and nurturing of our planet and its people. War, greed, violence, and suffering would have to end. It was a utopian ideal in opposition to the prevailing premise that nationalism was the only game in town and capitalism was the key to prosperity. Politically, Joseph McCarthy was looking for a communist around every corner, and the ideology promoted by our kindly space brothers and sisters was subversive. America and its allies were rebuilding after World War II, and the military in-dustrial state was in its infancy. Nuclear weapons had won the war and saved American lives. A new prosperity was founded in the exploitation of natural resources without concern for environmen-tal consequences.

Scientifically oriented UFO investigators, who were sometimes government connected, had an axe to grind with the purveyors of platitudes concerning the utopian life Earthlings could aspire to, if we chose to grow up and transform into a higher-minded soci-ety—one worthy of joining the Galactic Federation of spiritually enlightened planets. But it was not to be. Purveyors of this utopian message were collectively exposed as frauds and hucksters who were selling hope to credulous humans, not for the betterment of our planet, but for their own financial gain.

What we did not know is, beneath the surface, the US and Canadian governments were secretly investigating flying disks and the scientifically advanced telepathic messages that some people claimed they were receiving. Official policy called for UFOs to be stripped of the special status they had been given and the aura of mystery they had acquired. The plan was to reeducate the Ameri-can public to reduce its interest in the possibility of alien visitation. This was carried out by scientists, celebrities, and the media, who made laughing stocks out of those who claimed to have witnessed otherworldly craft, especially the contactees who were promoting contact with benevolent ETs.

This policy set the stage for our current trend toward the de-nial of all things extraterrestrial. It explains why you are reading this handbook instead of being helped by a government agency. Whether your contact experiences are positive, negative, or some-where in between, one thing is clear: there is no public funding available to assist anyone who is attempting to cope with their experiences. Despite evidence to the contrary, the mainstream scientific community does not believe your experiences are real. If you seek traditional medical help, you will probably be told that you have a psychiatric disorder. Volunteer organizations, such as the Mutual UFO Network (MUFON) and the Dr. Edgar Mitchell Foundation for Research Into Extraterrestrial and Extraordinary Encounters (FREE), are staffed by retired academics, scientists, lay researchers, caring volunteers, and experiencers like my coauthors and me. We fill this gap, but without the availability of funding, our scope is limited. One thing seems clear: if we are to understand the implications of modern contact, it is important for us to appreciate our history. The face of contact has evolved. Although some of its characteristics remain the same, it has become far more complex than any of us imagined.

The predominant notion that contact with extraterrestrials was benevolent and highly spiritual was demolished in 1966. A best-selling book, *The Interrupted Journey,* by John G. Fuller, stirred worldwide interest in a New Hampshire couple whose story of abduction set a new standard for contact. It became the historical model for contact with extraterrestrials because it involved the abduction of unwilling victims to an alien environment. We learned that abductees were subjected to mind control through telepathic communication, followed by intrusive medical procedures. Sometimes abductees would be given a tour of a technologically advanced craft. Some received information regarding the ET's home planet or warnings regarding the Earth's future if we continued to pollute our environment. Some abductees were shown catastrophic images of nuclear holocaust, tidal waves, volcanic eruptions, and earthquakes. These hapless victims were then returned to their natural environment, usually two hours later, with little memory of what occurred. Hypnotic techniques were developed to unleash the forgotten information lodged in a victim's subconscious mind and were used widely by researchers.

If we hope to understand modern contact, it is important to have insight into the past. The history of alien contact with humans is extremely important because it has built on and transformed the early abduction scenario. Let's review some of the significant cases that shaped our new understanding of contact with extraterrestrials and led to its evolution.

I will not dwell on the most famous case of alien abduction, as you might already be familiar with it. It involved an interracial, married couple from New Hampshire, who were returning to their seacoast home from a brief vacation in Canada, on September 19, 1961. At approximately 11:00 that evening, Betty Hill spotted a new object in the sky that seemed to be coming closer and closer. By 11:30 it swooped down and stalked the Hills' vehicle. By midnight they had a close encounter, at less than 200 feet, with a silent, hovering craft. Barney Hill picked up his binoculars and stepped from his car for an unencumbered view of the amazing vehicle. The craft dipped lower in the night sky, and something dropped down from its underside. Barney retained conscious recall of observing NHI entities through the craft's windows whose behavior caused him to fear for his life. He fled to his car, in a hysterical condition, repeating over and over that he and his wife had to get out of there or they were going to be captured. Shortly thereafter, he and Betty heard codelike buzzing sounds striking the trunk of their 1957 Chevy. A tingling sensation passed through their bodies, the car vibrated, and they entered into what appears to have been an altered state of consciousness. At least two hours passed before they were returned to US Highway 3 and became cognizant of their surroundings. They drove home to Portsmouth, but when they arrived, many things stirred their emotions. Physical evidence suggested that something had occurred during their

Betty and Barney Hill *(courtesy of Kathleen Marden)*

period of lost time. Disinterest turned to obsession and fear. The rest is history.

It was this close encounter with a silent, hovering "flying saucer" and the subsequent abduction of Betty and Barney Hill that set the prototype for what we have come to know as the modus operandi of alien abduction. After visual contact and an alteration in the victim's sense of reality came the onset of mental confusion, an electrical tingling sensation, and paralysis. Next came a period of missing time—usually about two hours.

The Hills' fleeting memories of encountering a roadblock and observing a fiery orb prior to being captured by aliens could not be successfully integrated into their conscious minds. How could it be? We knew nothing of alien intruders in 1961. Investigators speculated that the intensity of their trauma had caused dual amnesia for part of the alien and unearthly event. It was probably the powerful electromagnetic field that surrounded the craft and the entities themselves that led to a tingling sensation and the vague memories that nagged at the Hills.

In the Hill case, hypnosis by a medically licensed psychiatrist brought forth frightening information that had been lodged in their subconscious minds. These included a roadblock and face-to-face contact with NHI entities, described as being dressed in shiny black uniforms. Their hairless gray heads were larger than ours, and their penetrating eyes extended to the sides of their heads. They had large chests but walked on spindly legs. Communication was telepathic, except for an occasional *mmmmmmm* sound.

Barney's mind seemed to be under the control of one entity intent on moving their 1957 Chevy Bel Air to a desolate logging road. Or did they lift the Hills' car off the highway and relocate it onto the desolate logging road? We'll never know for certain. But one thing is clear: the Hills encountered a roadblock, and Barney brought his car to a halt. The motor died and the NHI entities approached their vehicle. When the couple realized the magnitude of what was occurring, Betty attempted to flee into the woods but was rendered unconscious. She awakened as she was being walked to a landed craft.

Barney had the sensation of floating, but he could feel his escorts' hands supporting him. He felt the toes of his shoes bumping along the rocky surface of a path through the woods. The path led to a landed disk. The couple was reassured that no harm would come to them before they were forced onto the craft and placed on examining tables. Next came intrusive medical examinations of their joints, skeletal structures, nervous systems, eyes, skin, hair, and mouths. The last procedure was demeaning for Barney and painful for Betty. It involved the removal of sperm and possibly ova.

Betty engaged in a conference with her escort and was shown a star map and strange symbols. When the NHI entities had completed their tasks, the couple was released to their natural environment. The Hills experienced approximately two hours of lost time that could not be accounted for in their autobiographical memories.

Physical and circumstantial evidence was collected and used to determine the authenticity of the experience. Betty's torn, discolored dress underwent laboratory analysis several times, all with anomalous findings. The trunk of their vehicle had new shiny spots in the location where the couple believed they had heard a series of codelike buzzing sounds. The following day, a physicist advised Betty to check her vehicle with a compass. When she and Barney held it over the newly discovered spots, the needle whirled, indicating a magnetic field. Barney's best dress shoes were ruined, and their watches never ran again.

The Hills were deemed credible by most of the scientists who investigated their case. They held stable jobs and filled an important role in their community. Betty passed a polygraph exam after Barney's death at age forty-six. But this evidence was not acceptable to the nuts-and-bolts skeptics who demanded an alien corpse or a crashed saucer. They offered strong opinions against alien abduction, especially after disinformants obfuscated the truth. These naysayers invented a new hypothetical timeline, altered the evidence in the historical record, and destroyed the witnesses' credibility. Betty endured their ad hominem attacks for the remainder of her life.

At this juncture, you might be shaking your head in disbelief. Your experiences do not resemble this archaic view of contact. Or perhaps some of the Hills' story rings true but seems primitive compared to what you have endured. The narrow scope of their captors' curiosity, the details pertaining to their examinations, the setting in which they were captured, and the three-dimensional nuts-and-bolts limitations of their experience seem foreign to today's experiencers. But the following paragraphs will help clarify the evolution of contact.

By the late 1960s the standard scenario had evolved slightly. Janet, a nineteen-year-old water skiing instructor, and Michael (pseudonyms), a local boy who took care of shore maintenance at the Buff Ledge Girl's Camp on Lake Champlain, Vermont, had a close encounter with a disk-shaped aerial object with pulsing, multicolored lights. Their sighting began at approximately 8:10 p.m. on August 7, 1968. At first, they saw a large cigar-shaped craft that released three smaller zigzagging craft. One of the craft approached the two as they stood on the camp's dock at sundown. Janet and Michael watched in amazement as the disk ascended vertically and then, in rapid descent, plunged into the lake. It emerged from the water and glided in a stair-step descent directly toward the dock where the couple was standing.

Now only sixty feet in the distance, the forty- to fifty-foot disk-shaped craft hovered above the water. An intense plasma-like light gleamed through its translucent dome. As it approached the mystified couple, Michael observed two slightly built, hairless figures, dressed in grayish or silver uniforms. His attention was drawn to their large, frog-like eyes that extended around the sides of their heads.

Janet fell into a trance while Michael communicated telepathically with the entities. They assured him that they intended no harm—they had come here long ago and returned to Earth after the detonation of our first atomic bomb.

When the craft was directly overhead, it emitted an intense cone-shaped beam, which engulfed the teens. It was approximately 8:30 p.m. when Michael instinctively grabbed Janet and hit the deck as he began to lose consciousness. As if only a moment had passed, they found themselves again on the pier. The disk was in a new location, hovering overhead, and the night sky had turned pitch black. The time was approximately 9:15 p.m., but it might have been later. There was a period of unaccounted-for time.

Ten years had passed when investigator Walter Webb received a phone call from Michael informing him of his close encounter and missing time event. Webb investigated the case and after a long search was able to locate Janet, who had moved to a southern state. Webb arranged to meet Janet during her scheduled visit to the Northeast.

As in the Hill case, the two witnesses underwent separate hypnosis by a qualified hypnotist, Harold Edelstein, DEd. His doctorate was in education, different from the credentials of the Hills' highly credentialed neuropsychiatrist, Dr. Benjamin Simon. Dr. Simon treated the Hills for trauma over a six-month period and used psychotherapy for the comfortable integration of their memories into their individual psyches. The focus of Michael and Janet's hypnosis sessions was memory retrieval. This became the subject of investigations by UFO organizations, often to the detriment of those who recovered memories of their alien abduction experiences.

In Michael and Janet's case, hypnosis revealed additional information about the NHI entities who inserted themselves into their lives. The entities' eyes had the appearance of a frog wearing racing goggles, with membrane-like lids. Their wider than tall greenish heads perched upon a thin neck. It became clear that they were not the gray NHI entities who abducted the Hills, although there were similarities. For example, their communication was telepathic.

Betty Hill had been shown a star map depicting a pattern of twelve circles connected by lines and eight pinpoint dots not connected by lines. The circles varied in diameter from nickel-size coins to pinpoints. Some of the lines were solid, depicting trade routes, whereas others were dotted, representing expeditions. In

1972, star map researcher Marjorie Fish identified the stars on Betty's map. The two major stars were identified as Zeta Reticuli 1 and 2, a wide binary system visible from the southern hemisphere.

This information was different from that communicated to Michael. He recalled being informed that these NHI entities were from Psi-Epsilon, an imaginary star system on *Star Trek*. This is typical of the confabulation that sometimes occurs during hypnosis, when the person does not have an autobiographical memory pertaining to a detail but feels pressed for information. Michael had told the hypnotist that he could not remember where the NHI entities claimed to be from. To this, the hypnotist firmly instructed Michael to remember immediately. When pressured for a name, Michael confabulated Psi-Epsilon. The hypnotist asked a series of direct questions that could have shaped Michael's recall, causing him to remember details incorrectly. Walter Webb's comparative analysis on the couple's separate statements revealed that they correlated 70 percent on the close encounter and 68 percent on the abduction experience. This result indicates that their hypnosis, much like memory itself, was effective for the retrieval of lost memories but was not entirely accurate.

As is common among physical experiencers, Michael described Janet's examination, by two NHI entities, while a third appeared to be monitoring test results on several screens. Skin, bodily fluid, blood, and ova samples were collected. Michael lost consciousness immediately after he was placed on a table, but Janet observed the entities carrying out his examination.

Michael began to have positive feelings toward one NHI entity with whom he communicated telepathically. He had the distinct impression that this NHI entity was in training and what the NHI learned might take lifetimes to divulge. Michael realized that this was not his own first experience. These strange NHI entities conveyed the message that they loved him and cared about him. Everything was going to be okay. They were friends of the Earth, who were from a distant place, but had been here always. They had returned to protect humankind from itself and the devastation caused by nuclear weapons. These supportive statements gave Michael an affinity toward his captors. He believed their mission was benevolent.

The 1970s and 1980s brought an exponential increase in the prevalence of alien abduction reports. I will not labor over the details in these well-known cases, but I will provide some important information that any experiencer should be aware of. The majority of these experiencers did not intentionally take their stories to the media. They were victims of circumstance and then suffered greatly at the hands of nasty skeptics and disinformants. The next well-known case offers a glimpse into the unfortunate consequences some experiencers endured when their experience was thrust into the media spotlight.

Most people who suspect they have had contact with extraterrestrials know of the Travis Walton case. He and six coworkers were returning home after laboring on a tree thinning contract in the Apache-Sitgreaves National Forest outside Heber, Arizona, on November 5, 1975, when their eyes were drawn to a glowing area up ahead. When they moved closer, they could see a flattened golden disk hovering only twenty feet or so above the ground. Impulsively, twenty-two-year-old Travis opened his door and walked toward the craft that was emitting a low humming sound. The sound amplified and the disk wobbled; then a blue-green beam shot out of its bottom and struck Travis, throwing him into the air and backward ten feet to the forest floor.

His coworkers panicked and fled, assuming that he had been killed, but realized they had a moral duty to rescue Travis or retrieve his corpse. When they could not find him, they reported the incident to the police, and when search crews could not find Travis, the coworkers came under suspicion of foul play. In an effort to prove their innocence, they submitted to polygraph examinations. The first three questions pertained to whether or not a crew member had harmed or killed Travis. The fourth asked if they had observed a UFO on the night that Travis disappeared. The lie detector results revealed that they were telling the truth. Only one of the six men faltered. He held a grudge against Travis and feared that the police would finger him as the perpetrator of a heinous crime. He walked out on the polygraph examiner before his test was completed.

Five nights later, Travis awakened on the side of a winding stretch of highway west of Heber and several miles from the site of his disappearance. The craft was ascending into the night sky and quickly disappeared from sight. Dazed and in a state of shock, he knocked desperately on a door, but no one came to his aid. He ran farther to a row of phone booths at an Exxon station and asked the operator to call his sister. Family members found him collapsed in the phone booth unaware that he had been missing for an extended period of time.

The terrified young man should have received emotional support through counseling and medication to relieve his anxiety. He would have benefited from quiet time with compassionate people who understood what he was going through. Instead, he hid at his brother's home in fear of being discovered by the media. They were already reporting that he had perpetrated a hoax. The media and skeptical UFO investigators did nothing but increase Travis's level of anxiety. A few compassionate investigators gave him assistance, but it was not enough given his situation. The director of the Aerial Phenomena Research Organization (APRO) compared Travis's emotional demeanor to that of a caged wildcat. How does one tame a caged wildcat? Certainly, he needed acceptance and support.

APRO arranged the funding for medical and psychological tests, hypnosis, and a polygraph exam through the *National Enquirer*. Travis underwent hypnosis for memory retrieval, but it was not of a therapeutic nature. Additionally, he submitted to a polygraph exam, but his extremely high level of anxiety and shock invalidated it. Later, he passed several lie detector tests.

Hypnosis by Dr. James Harder brought forth memories of Travis's abduction by two groups of entities. One group resembled the grayish entities described by Betty and Barney Hill and the other appeared human. For many years Travis suffered from his memories of alien abduction. But in recent years he has reasoned that the beam that threw him into the air might have caused grave injuries. He suspects that he was taken onto the craft as a rescue mission and might have otherwise died from his injuries.

As with all compelling cases of alien abduction, a disinformation campaign ensued. One ruthless go-to guy for the mainstream media impugned Travis's character and that of his family. This journalist proposed hypothetical scenarios meant to invalidate the truth, turning Travis into an LSD-crazed hoaxer and petty criminal out for a fast buck. When people close to Travis attempted to defend him, they were attacked and accused of wrongdoing. The youngest of Travis's coworkers claimed that he was offered $10,000 to expose Travis's story as a hoax. (See *Fact, Fiction, and Flying Saucers* by Stanton Friedman and Kathleen Marden for additional information.)

Only two months after the Walton abduction, three women from Kentucky were taken aboard a UFO. On January 6, 1976, shortly after 11:00 p.m., Louise Smith, Mona Strafford, and Elaine Thomas were driving home from a restaurant in Lancaster, Kentucky, when they saw a brilliant red object in the sky. Initially, it had the appearance of a plane on a collision course, but suddenly it stopped at treetop level. The women could now see a disk-shaped vehicle, with a glowing dome and red lights around the middle. It projected a blue-white light into the car, causing an electrical tingling sensation to pass through the women's bodies. Their car rose into the air, and they found themselves in an unearthly environment in the presence of four-foot-tall NHI entities who communicated telepathically. The women suffered physical and emotional effects, including anxiety, burning eyes, weakness, and burns on the back of their necks. They passed polygraph examinations and underwent hypnosis to elicit additional details pertaining to their event. The three women recalled undergoing painful examinations and experiments by telepathic, diminutive gray-skinned creatures, with large, dark eyes. But again, they faced criticism and doubt.

Many additional reports of alien abduction were made in this time frame. Most had witnesses to the craft, and some offered compelling evidence. However, the mainstream media sculpted their events in a manner that cast doubt upon their authenticity. The experiencers' mental health was brought into question, and prosaic explanations were advanced to ease the public's disquieting trepidation. Again, skeptics engaged in scathing criticism or offered dismissive explanations that simply did not conform to the evidence.

Denise Stoner and I were well versed on the arguments that had been advanced by debunkers and disinformants when I began an investigation of her experiences. Initially, she told me only about a period of missing time that she and her family had experienced in South Park Valley, Colorado. She requested anonymity and I guaranteed it.

I was drawn to her experience because it was similar to my aunt and uncle's missing time event in 1961. Denise was FL (Florida) MUFON's Chief Investigator and had worked on a national team of top investigators, so I knew she was level-headed and scientifically careful. Yet the story she told was staggering.

On August 13, 1982, Denise's husband, Ed, was behind the wheel of the family's two-tone Ford Granada wheeling toward their camping retreat near Buena Vista, Colorado. Denise and the family dog were in the passenger seat, and their daughter was asleep in the back seat. During the warm summer months, the family spent their weekends with Denise's parents and family friends at the Grace Acre Ranch. Denise's mother always had dinner awaiting their arrival at 8:00 p.m. or shortly thereafter.

The journey went like clockwork. Ed, Denise, and their daughter always left by 5:00 p.m. and filled their gas tank for the 137-mile drive. Sixty miles into their journey, Ed routinely stopped for a snack and to stretch his legs at a scenic overlook near the top of 10,000-foot high Kenosha Pass before he navigated the wide curved slope that ended on the valley floor near the small town of Jefferson.

As they descended from the pass, Denise's eyes were drawn to two bright yellow-white aerial lights that appeared to be moving rapidly in their direction. Four miles south of Jefferson, the lights moved over their vehicle, and the family immediately felt the sensation of being lifted sideways over a snow barrier and out over the high desert. Their next memory was of finding themselves at the other end of South Park Valley on Trout Creek Pass. The terrain was now blanketed in darkness, and a cold chill penetrated their bodies. They were forty miles south of their previous location, but they had no memory of how they arrived there or what had occurred during the previous two or three hours. Nor did their odometer indicate movement.

Frightened and confused, they wheeled into their summer encampment at nearly 11:45 p.m. Denise's parents were frantic and refused to believe their UFO story until they realized Denise and her family were in a near state of shock.

Ed and Denise chose not to report their perplexing experience, so they were spared the increased anxiety that always afflicts abductees when the media gets involved. It was a wise, well-thought-out decision, especially because Denise was employed by the National Park Service, and media attention could have jeopardized her job. My investigation began in 2010 and continues to this day. Denise has had a long history of contact with a group of Greys and Insectoids. (See *The Alien Abduction Files* by Kathleen Marden and Denise Stoner for Denise's story and Kathleen's investigation of six cases.)

Months into my investigation, I was astonished to learn that Denise believes she was only a toddler when she was first taken. This belief was confirmed by her mother, who spoke of being frightened when she and Denise's father saw what they thought was a plane flying on a collision course toward their Connecticut home. They had been preparing for bed, but this sight frightened them, so all activity stopped. They knew that they might have to gather their children and head for safer ground if the aircraft didn't change course and cease descending in their direction. Their next memory was of awakening to a new day. It is safe to assume that people in danger don't lie down in bed and fall asleep. It wasn't a conventional airliner on a collision course for Denise's childhood home.

Another of Denise's mother's perplexing experiences extended back to her own childhood. She and her young friend were playing in their neighborhood when they mysteriously lost track of time. Denise's mom entered into a state of altered consciousness and knew only that somehow she and her friend had regained conscious memory in an abandoned building that they hadn't entered. Shortly thereafter, her friend's family vanished. Her family told no one that they were leaving. As the stories of alien abduction built, it was becoming clear to me that theirs was generational, which our research has discovered is fairly common. We do not know if Denise's daughter, who has a disability, is a third-generation abductee, but she has some precognitive and psychic abilities that are uncannily common among experiencers.

I had a very strange experience with Denise on February, 2, 2013, that might have been an abduction, but I am not certain. She, my elderly father, and I had traveled to St. Petersburg, Florida, for a presentation by UFO photojournalist and investigative reporter Paola Harris. After her presentation, a group of us went to a nearby Greek restaurant for dinner. It was the type of no-frills eatery that offers fast service. We ordered our food at a counter, and it was delivered to our table. We left early for central Florida after saying our goodbyes to the group. The route was familiar to us, as we had traveled it several times in the past. We took I-4 to State Road 429, the fastest route to the Fowler Groves Mall in Winter Garden. Denise had parked her Hyundai SUV in the parking lot because it was halfway between my house and hers. The drive back from St. Pete normally took us an hour and fifty minutes to two and a half hours, depending on the traffic.

My 2011 Toyota Avalon delivered a comfortable, dependable ride every time. So, I was somewhat confused when my GPS instructed me to turn off I-4 onto a desolate side road. I immediately noticed that it had malfunctioned, so I reset it and continued on my drive. Denise, my father, and I were having a lively conversation about a variety of UFO-related topics when suddenly I felt as if my car were ascending up a steep hill. My next memory was of coming to a soft landing on the road. I thought to myself, "I must be very tired. I'm having perceptual difficulties." I didn't know until later that Denise was having an identical thought. She pointed out that my previously lively father was sound asleep in the backseat. I thought nothing of it at the time.

I continued on to the Fowler Groves Mall and dropped off Denise at her car in front of the Target store. She had intended to call her husband, but her phone had suddenly lost its charge. I hadn't turned on my flip phone, as I used it for emergency purposes only. It was fully charged, so Denise used it to advise her husband that she was on her way home. It was a fifty-minute drive to Denise's house and a thirty-five-minute drive for me. We bid each other farewell, and I headed home.

When Denise called me the following afternoon, I could hear tension her voice. It told me that something was very wrong. On her drive home from the Fowler Groves Mall, her fully charged insulin pump had completely discharged and was beeping an emergency signal. In addition to this, she had a major dashboard malfunction. But her primary concern was finding herself in a vaguely familiar location that she hadn't driven to. She suddenly realized that her car had stopped on a quiet road on the west side of Lake Baldwin, not on the highway she had been traveling on. She retained vague memories of a fiery orb rising up from the lake and of a familiar entity. She felt that the location was vaguely familiar, so she and another MUFON investigator had searched for and found it. Within a few days, I investigated the site. This was after I had my own weird experience.

It was Super Bowl Sunday, but I am not a football fan, so I spent the evening in my office conferencing with an experiencer in Australia. As soon as the game ended, I turned in for the night. My next memory was of awakening with a start with messages streaming into my mind. At first, I attributed it to a dream, as I had been working on a deadline for *The Alien Abduction Files,* my book with Denise, and had been struggling with the fatigue from overwork. Yet I was awake and the messages continued to flow into my mind. I thought of hypnopompic hallucinations, but that description didn't fit the bill. It seemed that I was receiving a rapid download of information. I had a vague memory of finding myself in an alien environment—a small, dimly lit room.

When I attempted to shift my position, my lower back and the left side of my head ached in pain. The pain was so intense that it hardly seemed worth turning over. I had no memory of injuring myself, so this was shocking! Had I been sleepwalking? Did I injure myself in a sleep state but remained in a deep sleep? As far as I know, I don't sleepwalk. My husband had not awoken. I had done nothing that could possibly account for the pain I was experiencing. Why was I experiencing the feeling that something dreadful had occurred?

As time went on, my curiosity got the better of me, so I arranged for Denise to come to my home and work with me in hypnosis. While tapping into my subconscious mind, I remembered the sensation of being jarred awake when I was dropped from above, coming down hard on a solid surface. I opened my eyes to a shocking scene. Inches from my face was the round, large head of a small Grey. His large eyes wrapped around to the sides, as if he were wearing silver-rimmed sunglasses. His face was flat and had an aluminum gray appearance. I wondered if he was robotic, except that I saw what might have been an expression on his face. I saw a tiny visible mouth with upturned corners. It was so thin that it appeared to have been penciled onto his face. Two familiar entities were standing near the foot of the table. The one off to my left was near my foot, and the other was at the end of the table. Both were taller than the small one and had smaller heads in proportion to their bodies. They admonished the small entity for making a mistake. I realized that something had gone wrong. Perhaps a mechanism used to transport me had malfunctioned and caused me to come down hard on their table. A haunting thought played in my mind. Was this intentional? Was it punishment for exposing their modus operandi in *The Alien Abduction Files?* But another message sprang forth: "That was an accident."

My next memory was of awakening in my bed. Information was streaming into my mind. I wanted to document it before it disappeared in a wisp of wind, but when I attempted to turn over, all I could focus on was the sting of pain. I would have dismissed this incident as a lucid dream if I hadn't been injured. What a way to confirm that Denise's memories of lifelong contact were probably real! I was in a state of shock and disbelief.

CHAPTER 1 QUESTIONNAIRE: HAVE YOU HAD A CLASSIC ABDUCTION EXPERIENCE?

Complete the following questionnaire to determine whether or not you've had a classic UFO abduction. By organizing your thoughts, you might remember more.

1. Have you observed a UFO?
2. Was it 500 feet or less away from you?
3. Do you remember seeing NHI entities?
4. Were you alone, or were other people with you? If other people were present, what do they recall?
5. Did you suddenly find yourself in a different location?
6. Have you experienced missing time while you were outside? If so, what do you recall?
7. Was there any evidence, such as marks on your body or a problem with your clothing?
8. Have you had recurring dreams about this experience?
9. Have you told anyone about your experience? If so, what was their reaction?
10. If other people ridiculed you, have you spoken with a nonjudgmental listener, such as a member of MUFON's Experiencer Research Team, who will not ridicule you?

Chapter 2

AM I AN ABDUCTEE?
A CONTACTEE? AN EXPERIENCER?

Kathleen Marden

Perhaps the uncertainty about whether you are an abductee, a contactee, or an experiencer—this feeling of doubt in your mind—has left a disquieting mark on you. You woke in the middle of the night unable to move and saw shadowy figures looming nearby. Your eyes glimpsed a funnel, blue and curved, in the corner of your room or on the ceiling above your bed. You felt energy coming from it, as if it were alive and had intelligence. Perhaps it enveloped you. Or maybe you watched as it receded into the distance. Maybe you were startled into wakefulness when you were gently dropped on your bed. Or perhaps your slumbering body sensed the mumbling presence of entities carefully tucking you in. This sense of confusion and uncertainty has probably affected all experiencers.

If you have read any of the skeptical literature on contact, you cannot help but wonder if your experience was real or only a sleep-related hallucination. Hypnagogic (between waking and sleeping) hypnopompic (between sleeping and waking) hallucinations, also called H/H hallucinations, occur when factors such as stress, extreme fatigue, medications, or mental illness cause the part of the brain that distinguishes between conscious perceptions and internally generated perceptions to misfire. This misfire results in internally generated visions, sounds, feelings, or tastes. H/H hallucination experiencers often see colored geometric shapes or parts of objects. Others might observe the full image of a person, monster, or animal. Sometimes lines or the outlines of figures are observed. Sensations of floating or flying are common, along with hallucinated buzzing sounds. H/H hallucinations can be frightening. They can last from seconds to minutes and are usually accompanied by a brief period of sleep paralysis. They are experienced as being as real, not as hallucinations or dreams. It is no wonder this state leaves confusion in the minds of those who suspect they have been contacted, or even abducted, by nonhumans.

If you have been able to determine through evidence or independent verification that you did not have an H/H hallucination, you might remain distressed for a while, as if you've experienced some kind of trauma. Your emotional pain usually diminishes as the days pass, but you are left with a nagging desire to learn more. If you have read the very frightening literature on alien abductions, you might continue to feel a high level of anxiety. Remember: just because someone else had a highly traumatic experience doesn't mean that you did. Contact can be positive, negative, or somewhere in between. An intense sense of curiosity will probably come to the forefront as your discomfort recedes.

I had this type of feeling for days and weeks after my fateful trip to St. Petersburg with Denise Stoner and my father. The burning desire to unlock the story behind my memories grew stronger with each passing day. I was well aware of the pitfalls of hypnotic regression and the uncertainty of recall when memories are retrieved using this tool, especially for a researcher like me who knows all of the intricate details of contact phenomena. But I had an overwhelming sense of curiosity. I had to know what happened in the presence of these strangely intense nonhuman entities. What was

Saturn-shaped UFO *(courtesy of Chad W., ERT)*

the content of the message that came streaming into my mind—too rapidly to recall? I called Denise and requested a hypnosis session. She drove to my office a few days later.

I told Denise everything I could recall about my fateful night, and moments later her voice lulled me into deep relaxation. I was immersed in the fabric of the soft hammock that was to be my escape route if the going got tough. It was like a soft cloud that would comfort me and keep me safe from my unfavorable memories. She deepened my hypnotic level, and I remembered Super Bowl Sunday as if it were yesterday. All of the details of the conversation with my friend in Australia emerged. The game ended, so I shut down my computer and kissed my elderly father good night. A short time later, my husband and I fell into a deep slumber.

I had no memory of seeing entities in my bedroom. The following day, however, my father spoke of strange activity and brightness outside his bedroom window. Memories began to emerge of the small, unfamiliar entity who inflicted my injuries, undoubtedly due to incompetence or inexperience. Two taller entities, by my feet, seemed vaguely familiar. I knew how displeased they were with the smaller one. They expressed concern about my injuries. For some reason, I thought that their little helper had made an excuse like, "Isn't she the troublemaker?" But it very well could have been my own speculation. (In early 2013 several experiencers told me they had been dropped, although I had not mentioned my experience to them.)

Denise gave me suggestions that reduced my pain and redirected me to what occurred next. She asked if I knew their purpose. What information could I glean from their presence? There was a review of what I had written in *The Alien Abduction Files,* my book with Denise, and how important it was for me to convey accurate information to others. Precision was of vital importance. There was so much more information that I couldn't comprehend. I knew only about their rapid transfer of information that was being downloaded into my mind when I awakened with a start. I still wonder if it was a dream, but a dream leaves me with no viable explanation for my injuries or the download of this valuable knowledge.

I told Denise that they are scientists with a job to do. We certainly don't understand why we're taken, but they stressed that no harm is being done. (Done to whom, I wondered.) They explained that taking me was just part of their program. It became clear to me that they were not making these decisions on their own. They were just working for the larger program, and these were the responsibilities they had to carry out as part of their job.

They stressed that they are sorry this is sometimes frightening, but they attempt to conduct their activities quietly without interfering too much in our lives. They're concerned about the hysteria and misinformation. Very frightening information is being disseminated that is making humans hostile toward them, when, in their opinion, there is really no valid reason for this hostility. It is based on falsehood. As a human being who had just been kidnapped and injured, I tried to understand their point of view. I wanted to forgive them. Then I thought of Josef Mengele from the Third Reich. My very human emotions rose to the surface.

I expressed concern for my fellow humans who felt traumatized and angry over being taken against their will and subjected to medical procedures without the opportunity to give consent. Why didn't they simply make their presence known and openly ask for human volunteers? They advised me that doing so would be too disruptive and might cause hostility. They said they were under orders from a higher source to continue as they have been, although some do show their craft from time to time. They made it known that other species are here as well—species who are not as concerned for humanity's welfare.

They wanted me to know that their group is attempting to upgrade human DNA, to move us ahead on an evolutionary scale. Our penchant for greed, our failure to be good stewards to our planet, our failure to care for our fellow humans, and our propensity for warlike behavior present a danger to the survival of our species. Our level of maturity is out of balance with our technological development and could lead us down the path to annihilation. They cautioned me that annihilation has happened before in our distant past and could happen again. This message made me feel a little more altruistic and sympathetic to their cause.

The reason for their shutdown of nuclear weapons facilities around the globe became crystal clear. It served as a warning to military leaders and heads of state. It is time to rein in military aggression before such aggression leads to an apocalypse. They have been sending out warnings to humankind since the 1950s, but few of us have listened. Will humanity's acknowledgment of their presence come too little and too late? They have given us a clear warning, but the dominant powers believe that people like you and me are delusional, fantasy prone, or experiencing H/H hallucinations. Will this ever change?

By closely monitoring family lines, they are able to document positive changes generationally. These alterations are also observable to other researchers and me. The offspring of generational experiencers tend to exhibit fascinating characteristics. Many are highly intelligent, empathic, intuitive, and compassionate. They seem mature beyond their years. Their benevolence is sometimes played out in their transformative ability to bring healing to others. Mary Rodwell, an Australian researcher, has documented these changes in her lectures and books. She calls her clients "the new humans," which is also the title of her book, *The New Human.* They are not selfish, hateful, or aggressive. Their primary concern is for our planet and the spiritual growth of their fellow humans.

This way of thinking was certainly not indicative of the behavior of the Greys described by Budd Hopkins and David Jacobs. Had I confabulated? Is this a grand deception? Budd's words to me resonate repeatedly in my mind. "Kathy, never trust an alien." Dr. John Mack held a different, more spiritual point of view. Budd gave his clients the label *abductees,* whereas John Mack invented the more generic term *experiencers.* Others who have engaged in highly spiritual, positive contact have been called *contactees* since the early 1950s.

In 2016, Suzy Hansen's book *The Dual Soul Connection: The Alien Agenda for Human Advancement* offered similar benevolent claims. In addition, I had recently spoken at California's mega-UFO event, "Contact in the Desert," where I had the opportunity to discuss my information with other researchers and experiencers. Sherry Wilde, a real estate agent from Wisconsin, told her story of lifelong interaction with beings from another world. From the stage at the open-air amphitheater, she spoke of her journey beyond fear, to understanding and purpose.

Sherry's story had the ring of truth that resonated deep into my personal history. I realized that I had no good reason to be fearful. Yet, the idea that people like me might simply have Stockholm Syndrome—a tendency for a hostage to bond with, sympathize with, or have positive feelings toward their captors—should not be discounted. Academic testing indicates that I have UFO Abduction Syndrome—the emotional signature and knowledge related to alien abduction. But somehow, I have been transformed. I have a greater level of understanding than ever before.

I'm not preaching. I'm reflecting on my own personal journey from terror to acceptance and spiritual growth. You may not be there yet. Or perhaps your experiences have been of a different tone, more like those described as caring little for humans.

There is a movement among some of today's researchers to label all experiencers *contactees*. I strongly disagree. You are entitled to your own memories, whether they are positive, negative, or somewhere in between. It is not ethical for others to impose their beliefs on you. To do so usurps your autonomy and belittles you as a person. No one should disregard your trauma by stating that all contact is positive. Nor is it acceptable to label you "immature" because you do not love your nonhuman contacts, abductors, or invaders.

Sometimes entities intrude into people's lives, take what they want, and leave their helpless prey in a perpetual state of terror. I will not deny the fact that it is completely acceptable for people to develop beliefs and attitudes that are consistent with their emotional experiences. Many people are angry because they have been taken against their will. It is a violation of their human rights. Whether or not it is an altruistic endeavor for the ultimate benefit of humanity is a moot point when one's predominant human rights are being violated.

Matt (a pseudonym) shared this state of mind when he contacted me in 2014. He had seen me on television and hoped that I could help him cope with the frightening entities that had inserted themselves into his life and held him in a state of terror. UFO and paranormal investigators had flocked to his residence, but the magnitude of his problem seemed overwhelming. He felt that no one believed him. This belief sent up a warning flag telling me that he might be delusional. Some people lack credibility. Was he simulating an abduction experience for attention? Did he hope that I could land him a job on a reality TV show? A little investigation brought forth evidence that one UFO investigator had observed an unconventional aerial vehicle close up at Matt's residence in 2010. This information provided the independent verification that I needed.

I was busy with a new book and speaking engagements, so I referred Matt to my team at MUFON—the Experiencer Research Team. I hoped that my colleague Dr. Michael Austin Melton, a retired clinical psychologist, could assist Matt through understanding, guidance, and a referral to a therapist who specialized in alleviating the symptoms of post-traumatic stress disorder. But Matt felt that he'd worn out his welcome with UFO and paranormal investigating groups. He didn't follow through.

Matt resurfaced in 2015, and this time I took notice. He had thousands of photos and videos for analysis, but no one had the time to search through that many photographs. I asked him to send me his ten best photos. I received about five dozen. This gave me some insight into why investigators had lost their patience with him. Most of his pictures showed nothing significant. But among the blurry and unremarkable were several clear photos of structured craft that I found intriguing. By 2016, we had communicated with one another 248 times.

Matt's case was both complex and perplexing. I learned that he had been a commercial pilot for twenty-nine years and, in 2008, entered into his business at a small airport in the southwestern United States. He and his wife lived in an apartment at his business but planned to eventually build a house on adjacent property. The airport property was located on former tribal land that he said had been donated to the county. The airport was surrounded by timber company land. No one lived within two miles east, west, or north of the airport. It was in a desolate and heavily wooded area.

Prior to 2010, Matt had never observed a UFO, nor was he interested in the topic. All of this changed one night when he heard activity on his runway. He had been working late in his shop, so he stepped outside to investigate. Five people were gathered together pointing toward the southeast. They watched as a bright, pulsating light went zipping through the sky and stopped over the town, a couple of miles from their location. It appeared to be accompanied by another craft about 10,000–15,000 feet above it that gave the appearance of thousands of little lights, with a central area that wasn't illuminated. The light was the purest and cleanest Matt had ever seen—whiter than white. *Angelic* was the word that popped into his mind.

The idea of extraterrestrial visitation became so captivating that Matt read everything he could find on the Internet regarding CE-5 contact experiments. (CE-5 contact experiments are defined as an individual's or group's attempt to attract UFOs for the ultimate purpose of contact with NHI entities. Groups around the world are currently engaging in contact attempts.) Then he devised his own method. First, he used an old US Navy signal/searchlight to send messages in Morse code. This approach had limited success, but he thought that a few objects had flashed back at him. Investigators suspected that the flashing was autokinesis, the illusion of movement or a twinkling effect caused by the human eye's response to staring at a stationary object, or refraction and dispersion, when a star seems to twinkle or change color due to changes in uniformity as it shines through the atmosphere. Matt disagreed.

A few days later, he concocted a new method. This involved buying 500 feet of red rope lighting and then attaching the lighting to precut two-by-fours and setting it up like a giant arrow pointing to a green circle with an X in the center. He thought this signal would surely entice them to land. But this approach, too, failed to lure in unconventional craft.

Matt's greatest hope was to meet face to face with extraterrestrials—to sit down and have a chat. He devised new methods of attracting their attention, using laser lights. He purchased two red and green 200 MW laser pointers and had several 35 MW helium-neon red laser tubes, with power supplies. This method attracted their attention, and they soon began to show up on a regular basis. Matt told me that they did not like being hit by one of those lights. He wasn't sure why, but he tried it half a dozen times and received "a violent response" from the craft he struck. He said the craft would immediately drop altitude and make a beeline straight to where he stood, flashing multicolored lights extremely fast. Matt's final laser light experiment resulted in injuries that caused his nose and ears to pour blood and the most severe headache he had ever experienced. He could barely get back inside his building without losing consciousness.

Matt soon realized that although he had attracted the attention he yearned for, it was not on his terms, and he could not exert control over when it occurred. Initially, he had been shooting photos of the unusual craft he had attracted with power lasers. When he realized that he was not able to control his level of contact, he attempted to drive them away with deadly weapons. He spoke of the *ping* that some of his bullets made when they hit his target, whereas other craft did not appear to have mass. Although he could see them and their image registered on his photographs, some of them would dive into the ground and disappear without a trace.

One of Matt's first encounters with a craft was late one winter's night. The hangar was shut down, and he had been in his office finishing paper work. It was late; he guessed between eleven and midnight. He had gathered together the day's office trash and walked across the hangar to an unlocked door. Trash bag in hand, he stepped

Matt's landed UFO *(courtesy of MUFON)*

out onto the ramp and walked to a dumpster behind the hangar. No sooner had he tossed the trash bags in than his eyes met a sight that nearly caused him to faint. An estimated eighty-five feet in the distance was a long black object, shaped like a hot dog bun, with a band of lights around its perimeter. Matt froze in his tracks while he gathered the courage to approach it. Finally, he walked slowly toward it.

He ran his index finger over its smooth-as-glass surface, and when nothing happened, he began to walk slowly around it. He searched for seams, fasteners, anything that would allow him to gain access to its interior, but he found nothing. He then noticed that it wasn't resting on the ground. It was hovering about three feet above the ground. This thing looked like glass, except that it was approximately twenty feet wide, ten feet tall, and around eighty feet long.

He assumed that no one would believe his story of a landed craft, so he eased away from the hovering rectangle and headed for his apartment. He quickly grabbed his camera and tripod and headed back toward the remarkable object that was resting above the ground near his small hangar. As he exited the main hangar, he reached for the light switch and turned on the ramp lights. He stepped back out onto the ramp and scanned the area for the exact location of the craft, but it was gone.

Matt's was the only business that had ever been located on the field, and if he found himself in a dangerous situation, the seconds counted. For this reason, he patrolled his property each night on the lookout for rowdy teenagers who might get a kick out of damaging his runway lights or otherwise vandalizing his property. One night, as he reached the north end of the runway, roughly three-fourths of a mile from the hangar, he stopped to take out his handheld spotlight, when his eyes met a huge lime green ball. It had the appearance of rolling, boiling plasma. It shot across an opening between the trees and the runway, hovering thirty feet or so overhead. In a state of panic, Matt grabbed his AR-15 and dumped the entire thirty rounds into it. As he fired, the ball began zipping back and forth, but only moving its overall width from left and right. Even though he was close to it, it dodged every round, leaving him standing there with his mouth wide open, feeling defenseless.

He learned a valuable lesson that night: our crude technology was absolutely no match for these things. He finally stopped carrying anything but a camera, reasoning that if it had wanted to kill him, there was nothing he could have humanly done to stop it. With every contact made, the more amazed he became at their abilities and how advanced their technology seemed. With this came increased contact, and before long, this contact moved to the next level.

One night, after Matt had fallen into a deep sleep, a strange noise suddenly snapped him into full consciousness. His alarm clock read 4:00 a.m. He had never heard this sound before, so he decided to investigate but found nothing unusual. He then went to his kitchen for a glass of water. Glass in hand, he started to head back to bed but realized that he was fully awake, so he decided to call his sister, who worked overseas. Soon he was pacing slowly back and forth in the living room, as he and his sister caught up on their personal lives and family news. After ending their conversation and without giving it any forethought, Matt walked to his apartment door, opened it, and glanced down into his shop below. What happened next made him wish that he had never attempted to contact what he assumed were extraterrestrials.

He had already taken a step out toward his shop when there standing before him were two tiny entities. Their three to three-and-a-half-foot tall frames suddenly swiveled toward him like a gate, startling Matt greatly. They moved together in perfect unison. Their bald heads appeared slightly out of proportion to their bodies, and their large glistening eyes glared in his direction. He remembered that their somewhat translucent skin had a light bluish tint, and each was dressed in identical metallic silver jackets and trousers with matching roper-style boots. (Although the attire that these entities were wearing is unusual, it has been reported in other entity sighting cases.)

Matt noticed a third entity facing his eastern wall that swiveled around to face him in a very disturbing way. It stood about his height—maybe six feet. Although it appeared to be completely naked, Matt saw no genitalia. Nor did it have nipples. Its smooth skin was a bark tan color. The back of its head was larger than the front, and its eyes looked like two protruding softballs. When the creature blinked, its eyelids met in the middle. This is what Matt remembered observing before he turned on his heel and hightailed it into his apartment, securing the deadbolt lock behind him. I suspect that they went straight through the door after him, but Matt remembered nothing more.

Thereafter, Matt began having repeated contact with these non-human entities. He felt it was strange that they spoke English, yet there was no visible movement of their mouths. He cautioned me that he was aware he sounded insane, but it was as if he could hear them in his head. This way of thinking indicates his level of naivety with regard to these telepathic entities, unless he was lying in order to deceive me. In the history of human contact with NHI entities, there rarely is any mention of vocalizations from them, although there have been reports of mumming, zipping, and grunting sounds. He felt amazed that they could hear what he was thinking almost before he could get the words out. He couldn't remember many details. It was almost like a dream. He seemed to remember always being in the shop that was between his apartment and the main hangar when they would intrude into his reality.

One day, he discovered dirt, debris, and blades of grass embedded in his window, which led him to suspect that they had passed through it. He also became aware of periods of lost time that he simply could not account for. One night he went to the restroom, washed his hands, and headed back to work. When he glanced at the clock, it was almost eleven. He was certain that it had been half past six when he headed for the restroom and was convinced that he had not fallen asleep. He said it was difficult to describe the confusion he felt. Over four hours had passed in the blink of an eye. This is when he began to question his own sanity.

One night he was sound asleep when he awoke with a start. The first thing that struck him was that he was totally frozen in bed. He couldn't move a muscle. Strangely, he was able to focus his eyes on a humanoid figure standing at the foot of his bed. It stood at least six feet tall. Its head was devoid of hair, and its huge almond-shaped eyes covered most of its face. Its nose was barely noticeable—just a small ridge with two holes for nostrils. Its mouth amounted to no more than a slit. There were no lips. Its tan-colored skin appeared to be no different from what he had seen on other humans.

By this time, Matt was determined to drive these menacing entities away by any means possible. It was his nightly habit to sleep with his Glock 17 in his right hand, rounds in the chamber. He could not fall asleep without the feel of the knurled grip in his palm.

As he lay screaming in his mind at the horror that this apparition posed, he mentally forced his right hand up and squeezed off a round, hitting it dead center. It doubled over and then disappeared in a blinding blue burst of light. Matt immediately jumped out of bed and turned on the lights. Spattered on his bedroom floor and the foot of his bed was a yellow substance. Since he knew of no laboratory that could analyze it, he did not collect a sample for analysis.

This evidence would have been an investigator's dream. By this time, though, his investigators had gone their separate ways, and he hadn't contacted me yet. Matt was convinced that no one believed him—that he was facing these incredibly disturbing phenomena alone.

Soon, new activity of a decidedly paranormal nature began to pervade Matt's life. There were ghostly apparitions and time slips. Fortunately for him, he was not alone when he observed them. This gave him confirmation that he was not hallucinating or delusional. He and others watched in wonder as one hysterical translucent woman, in a torn dress and holding an infant, came into view. Two women had been killed in crashes at the airport, and Matt wondered if this was one of them.

One night he and his mother observed a grassy savannah and grazing mammoths at the end of his runway. This phenomenon occurred after his family staged an intervention to force him into psychiatric treatment. He requested the chance to prove that he was not hallucinating or delusional, so his mother had agreed to spend the night at his apartment. I have interviewed another family member and a friend who confirmed that Matt was a solid, intelligent man who was being subjected to real intrusions. They had witnessed them in Matt's presence.

Finally, after a year of intense harassment, he could tolerate it no longer. He felt as though he was being assimilated into this living hell on earth, and the NHI entities were doing it to him at night while he slept. He and his employees sometimes glimpsed at their presence in the early evening from the open hangar. He was living under siege and felt tired and mentally defeated. Suicidal thoughts were beginning to pervade his mind. Horrific nightmares became a nightly issue. He said it was like being in a different *Twilight Zone* show every night. The entities that he had invited into his life would not let him rest.

After the time Matt found himself more than a mile away from his apartment at daybreak, he knew that he had to take action. He tried remaining awake instead of sleeping, but by the third day he felt like a babbling idiot. This is when he decided to search the Internet for methods to end abduction. He locked himself in a small bedroom with three-quarter-inch plywood fastened over the window and a handcuff that he had modified with a six-foot chain bolted to the wall. It gave him reasonable comfort and allowed him to sleep through the night. Before he turned in, he sprinkled baby powder on the floor around his bed, knowing that it might show footprints if entities disturbed him during the night. Finally, he was granted a reprieve and the restful sleep that he so badly needed.

One night, Matt was fast asleep when he was awakened by a female voice calling his name. The room was filled with a brilliant bluish-white light. Standing facing the east wall of his apartment was what looked like an angel with black hair. She was dressed in a glowing, white, floor-length robe. Matt believed that she was preventing a belligerent, naked man, with shoulder-length black hair, from entering through the wall. By this time, Matt had returned to his Catholic roots and thought she was his guardian angel trying to protect him from evil. The security camera that he had mounted on his wall captured fifty or sixty photos of the entire event, which lasted until the sun began to rise.

After a year or so, Matt began to see part of these objects and the entities they carried as not some race of beings thousands of years ahead of us from some far-flung galaxy. He started seeing what could only be described as EVIL. He photographed an entity that resembled a humanoid figure with a wolf-like head. Then one night as he walked across a grassy area that separated his facility from the runway, he was attacked by something unseen. He saw the damage as it was done but could not feel or see what was attacking him. He needed thirty-six stitches to close his gaping wound.

Matt began to see goat heads inside floating orbs and entities with faces that resembled baboons. Equipment shot off shelves and flew through the air. Matt was working at his table one night alone when he felt as if someone had hit him in the chest with a hot poker. He ran for his mirror and saw three red lines forming, as if something invisible was burning three parallel lines across his chest. It was a month before they completely healed.

He couldn't stop this decidedly evil activity, nor could he protect himself. An arsenal of weapons could offer no protection against his tormentors. He traded in his weapons for rosary beads and took communion on a regular basis. Yet, no matter what he did, the highly negative activity continued. When nothing eased his pain, he attempted to leave his airport.

Matt loathed this evil and what it did to him. It took away his job, his home, his reputation, and his wife. It left him destitute and unsure of what to do. His confidence was shattered, and he didn't know who to turn to. It created enemies where before there had been none. It drove a spike between him and his family. Matt had prided himself in how well he had walked the line, being a good loyal American taxpayer and citizen. Forgetting that he had invited this madness into his life, he felt that this evil had attacked him without provocation. Formerly a robust forty-eight-year-old, he was now in failing health. He developed heart problems and kidney failure. Each time that he attempted to flee his airport, he would fall deathly ill. He was rushed to the hospital with organ failure. Finally, he was able to escape from the living hell that he had brought upon himself. But he was a shell of the man he had once been.

I have only touched upon the horrific situation that Matt faced when he naively called in what he believed were extraterrestrial entities from a highly advanced planet. The beings that he invited into his life were nothing of the kind. They did not fit the modus operandi or the behavior of spiritually advanced beings who were attempting to assist in humanity's development, or beings who had enlisted humans to assist in the continuation of their species. They appear to have been highly negative interdimensional entities, perhaps of a demonic nature, from the astral plane or residing under the Earth's surface.

I have spoken with others who called entities to themselves, believing that they would become spiritually or intellectually enlightened. Few achieved their goal. Negative entities attached to them, and more often than not, they could not disengage themselves from these intrusive beings. Only a shaman, a religious figure trained in exorcism, a light worker, or a team of people who specialize in the removal of entity attachments can be of assistance when this situation occurs. It appears to be a case of oppression and could lead to possession if no intervention is carried out.

I suspect that a variety of things occurred in Matt's case. His initial sighting of an unconventional craft might have been of nonearthly, perhaps extraterrestrial, origin. Based on my years of research and investigation, I conjecture that most ETs possess interdimensional technology that can open portals. If I am correct, the portal over Matt's airport was not closed. When Matt called in entities that made his life a living hell, the portal offered a passageway for negative interdimensional entities and human spiritual entities to enter. It can also account for the time-space discontinuity that Matt and his mother observed.

Matt requested assistance from paranormal and UFO investigators who did not understand the complexity and malevolence of his situation. My effort to assist him was not successful. I attempted to involve an ordained minister/spiritual counselor who has the ability to banish demonic attachments and is a seasoned paranormal investigator. The minister/spiritual counselor and I entered into a period of prayer prior to our appointment, but Matt was not there at the appointed time. He had been rushed to the hospital. Not long thereafter, he perished.

Please do not attempt to invite nonhuman entities into your life unless someone with a highly positive connection is there to assist you. Even then, if you live in fear and loathing, you can attract negative entities who feed off negative human emotions. I often wonder if this is a battle between good and evil. Are these entities not highly advanced extraterrestrials, but instead the forerunners to the return of the Messiah? I cannot answer this question.

Clearly, not all contact experiences are equal. Mine were initially terrifying, but after years of contact, they became highly positive. I assume that my contact experiences are generational because my aunt and mother were experiencers. However, I have no recall of participating in the hybrid program. My participation has been for the benefit of humanity and to communicate their overriding concern that malevolent humans have brought a negative collective consciousness to this planet that could lead us to destruction on a grand scale. They assert that they are extraterrestrial in origin and here to give guidance to humanity. They declare that negative human thought from our collective consciousness gives life to negative parasitic entities and demons. We must engage in positive thought and look within if we hope to avoid the negativity that is increasingly pervasive on our planet.

Matt's contact experiences were decidedly negative and sometimes evil. However, when he called out to a higher power, a light being that he identified as an angel protected him. Modern technology recorded the event on camera. I do not believe that Matt perpetrated a hoax. I have received many reports that lead me to believe malevolency has infested a portion of the Southwest. People are suffering. You can help by being pure of mind and positive in thought. Transcend your base human emotions and look beyond yourself and into yourself. Find peace within and work toward elevating your thoughts and emotions. Honor your religious beliefs and live within the moral code and ethical guidelines you believe in. Religion and spirituality are not mutually exclusive unless your religious doctrine instills fear rather than hope, hatred rather than brotherhood, and exclusion rather than inclusion. Love your fellow human. Above all, if you are suffering and want relief, read Chapter 10. It offers a variety of suggestions that have worked for others.

CHAPTER 2 QUESTIONNAIRE: GATHER YOUR THOUGHTS AND SET YOUR PRIORITIES

Use this questionnaire to help you gather your thoughts about your own experiences. Do you have the symptoms of sleep paralysis or abduction paralysis? Do you want to pay a hypnotist or hypnotherapist to facilitate your memories? If so, what type of hypnotist would you like to visit? Are your experiences more like Kathleen's or Matt's? There are no right or wrong answers here. The intent is to facilitate your thought processes as you think about the nature of your own experiences. (You'll find Kathleen's comments below.)

1. Have you awakened paralyzed and unable to move anything except your eyes?
2. Have you been awake and moving when someone unknown entered your bedroom and you suddenly felt electrical tingling followed by paralysis?
3. Have you awakened paralyzed and observed partial figures in your bedroom such as the face of an alien, part of an animal, geometric shapes, or numbers?
4. If you are thinking about undergoing hypnosis to facilitate your memories of a contact experience or experiences, what type of hypnosis do you want?
5. Would you travel to see a highly skilled hypnotherapist?
6. Why wouldn't you make it easy on yourself and see your local hypnotist or have a friend do it?
7. You've heard a lot about regression therapy. What is it?
8. Why do you think the ETs were concerned about the information that Kathleen had written in *The Alien Abduction Files?*
9. Do you think they can be believed?
10. What about their claim that they are upgrading the human race to a higher level? Do you believe them?
11. Will you forgive them for taking you and your family if it is for the benefit of humanity?
12. Why do you think that Kathleen placed little weight upon being dropped?
13. Do you think that her affection for the NHI is real or caused by manipulation?
14. Do you believe that your experiences are positive or negative?
15. How did Kathleen's experiences differ from Matt's?
16. Do you think that the NHI entities who intruded into Matt's life were ETs?
17. Why do you think they were ETs, or why do you think they were something else?
18. If you were Matt, how would you have handled the intrusions differently?
19. If you were injured during a UFO sighting, would you continue to pursue contact?
20. Do you think that the NHI entities who intruded into Matt's life were demons? Why or why not?

CHAPTER 2 QUESTIONNAIRE: COMMENTS

1. If you answered "yes," you have a classic symptom of sleep paralysis. It may or may not indicate that something more complex is occurring.

2. If you answered "yes," you have a classic symptom of alien abduction. Your body is being prepared to transport you to an alien environment.

3. A "yes" answer indicates that you have a classic symptom of sleep paralysis.

4. Forensic hypnosis will facilitate the recall of memories without the hypnotist leading. But do you want more? Would you prefer the healing effects of therapeutic hypnosis? Would you like to accomplish both? Speak with your hypnotist before you make an appointment to determine what will be accomplished and what is right for you.

5. You'll have to consider your priorities. If you are concerned about cost, you might not want to pay travel expenses, hotel costs, car rental, and so on, especially if you will have to make multiple trips to a distant location. You might be tempted to have online hypnosis, but it is unethical and could endanger you. Perhaps you can arrange a hypnosis appointment at a UFO conference, such as IUFOC or Roswell. Some well-known hypnotherapists offer their services and support groups at conferences. See Appendix A for suggestions.

6. Be certain that your hypnotist or hypnotherapist is certified or licensed and is experienced in working successfully with experiencers. Special techniques and knowledge are required. Don't become a victim. Would you ask your friend or an unqualified person to pull your tooth? To perform surgery on you? Your peace of mind is of utmost importance.

7. Hypnotic regression means going back through the subconscious memory to find and tackle events in your past that might be contributing to your problems in the present. Your treatment will focus on resolving past events that are contributing to your current level of anxiety. This treatment is controversial because it might enhance false memories. Since it is therapeutic and time consuming, a licensed psychotherapist is the best choice if you really want to express and release the emotions linked to your trauma. It will require reprogramming your subconscious mind by working through your emotional responses to your events.

This approach also can be costly. Certified hypnotists have developed streamlined methods of avoiding painful memories and trauma. This involves age regression where events from the past are recalled as if they were occurring in the present time. Certified hypnotists and hypnotherapists are not licensed mental health practitioners. Therefore, they cannot legally carry out therapeutic psychotherapy. However, much healing can be accomplished using hypnotic techniques.

8. Kathleen thinks the NHI entities are concerned about being misrepresented. Human emotions run high during the abduction process. The fight-or-flight response shifts into full gear. Panic is dominant. Horror induces high emotions and is promoted for the purpose of making huge media profits. The benevolent NHI entities are very concerned about falsification for profit. Would you want to be transformed into a monster by a promoter of a negative agenda?

9. Kathleen believes their messages, but she is a positive, nonviolent, respectful person. Those who choose violence and promote their own controlling agenda will disagree with Kathleen. Each of us is entitled to our own thoughts and emotions. No one knows the absolute truth, but some people promote themselves and their agenda as if they do. These people tend to perceive the world as black and white, without considering the many shades of gray (no pun intended).

10. Dating back to the 1950s, experiencers of physical and nonphysical contact have reported the same concerns. NHI entities do not want to interfere with human development, but they do want to ensure the survival of the human species. They fear that human behavior will lead to planetary extinction. Some claim to have seeded life on our planet and are the caretakers of Earth.

11. Again, this is an individual choice. Try sending telepathic messages to your NHI entities. Ask them to explain their reason for taking you. If you want it to stop, see the suggestions in Chapter 10.

12. Kathleen wants to believe that being dropped was an accident. Several experiencers have reported apparent equipment malfunctions that caused minor injuries. Just as we are not perfect, they are not without mistakes.

13. Kathleen believes that she is not a victim of Stockholm Syndrome. Your own memories and past experiences will shape your response.

14. Your experiences are your own. Make a list of your positive contact memories. Then make a list of your negative memories. Which outweighs the other?

15. Kathleen's memories are positive and accepting, whereas Matt's were negative and induced great suffering. They experienced entirely different phenomena. Kathleen's NHI entities were scientific and reassuring. Matt encountered negative, shapeshifting interdimensionals. These beings attached themselves to his aura and fed off his negative emotions. He suffered greatly, whereas Kathleen suffered fear until her understanding increased.

16. They did not assume the modus operandi of ET NHI entities.

17. Perhaps Kathleen's analysis of the two situations is incorrect. Perhaps you will come to a different opinion. The absolute truth is out of reach.

18. Matt acted on his emotions. His initial interest and destructive behavior caused the negative interdimensional NHI entities to build energy and inflict greater damage. This type of war—spiritual war—cannot be won with weapons. A spiritual specialist, such as a shaman, priest, light worker, or rainbow worker must be called in.

19. Again, this decision is a matter of personal choice. If your contact is negative, dispose of it before it grows and inflicts greater harm. Kathleen works with several middle-aged men who are seeking relief from negative, interdimensional attachments that have turned their lives into a living hell. See Chapter 10 for suggestions.

20. If you concluded that they are not of ET origin, you are correct. Highly negative entities from the astral plane can masquerade as ETs, but their behavior is markedly different.

Chapter 3

HOW TO INVESTIGATE YOUR CONTACT EXPERIENCES

Kathleen Marden

Imagine a perfect world where experiencers could be absolutely certain that their memories of encounters with nonhuman intelligent entities are real—where the NHI entities pose for photos and display their craft, with you standing in the window, waving to the photographer below. Unfortunately, we do not live in a perfect world, and the entities who have contacted you prefer not to reveal themselves to humanity. For our benefit or for their own benefit, they choose to remain in the shadows, appearing to only a few. For this reason, many experiencers are driven to documenting their own contact experiences for their own knowledge and peace of mind.

How do you document such fleeting experiences? What are the protocols for collecting evidence? And what can be considered valid? MUFON's Experiencer Research Team, of which I am the director, makes several recommendations to those who contact us at *www.mufon.com* and visit the ERT's page. We ask those who are seeking assistance to complete the Experiencer Questionnaire. You'll find the link at the top of our page. It will take you to the questionnaire, where you will be asked to read the instructions, then provide your name, email address, city, state, and country, and whether or not you wish to be contacted by a member of the ERT. I wrote the instructions for an important reason: I want you to know that your score has little significance. However, your answers pave a path to the type of conversation a specialist will initiate with you. Please read the instructions before you answer the thirty questions on the questionnaire. They are as follows:

> You may suspect that you have been visited by nonhuman entities and are seeking additional information with regard to your experience. Or perhaps you have conscious recall of a contact experience or alien abduction and would like to find a support group or a qualified hypnotherapist. Perhaps you'd like to speak with a nonjudgmental person who will listen and not criticize. Or perhaps you've had an experience and are wondering if you should report it to MUFON for a possible investigation. MUFON's ERT can assist you with all of these matters. Your identity will remain anonymous.

The general questions of the Experiencer Questionnaire may or may not pertain to your experiences. You might find that many of them do. A high score does not necessarily indicate that you have been contacted by nonhuman entities, nor does a low score indicate that you have not been contacted. The score merely gives the ERT an indication of what you have in common with other experiencers and serves as an icebreaker when you begin your conversation with a member of MUFON's ERT.

You would be surprised at the percentage of people who request contact by an ERT specialist but then do not follow through when they receive an email message that can initiate a conversation via the telephone or Skype. Perhaps they lose their nerve. Or perhaps they fear criticism. Maybe they have heard the false rumor that

MUFON will give their information to a government agency. It won't. Team members have been trained to engage in nonjudgmental listening. They are there to offer you help. Some of our members are experiencers. Others have worked in a supportive role with experiencers. They will not make a decision regarding the veracity of your experiences. This is your job. However, they can give you some guidance. In 2017, the ERT received 1,290 completed questionnaires. This figure increased to 1,383 questionnaires in 2018. About 50 percent spoke with an ERT member.

ERT members do not offer therapeutic services. Although some of our members are retired therapists, they are no longer working in this field. They are trained volunteers who care about you enough to offer a modicum of assistance, so you won't be left feeling helpless and without the information you need to move forward. MUFON does not have funding to pay for your medical expenses or for hypnosis. We maintain a list of vetted professionals who offer services to experiencers, but you must pay for your own hypnosis, medical treatment, professional counseling, DNA testing, blood tests, surgery, and so on.

Many experiencers have the erroneous impression that MUFON has a team of hypnotists standing by to facilitate their memories, in exchange for information, and without charge. This idea is false and is rooted in the past. Years ago, many self-styled hypnotists worked with abductees, at no charge, as part of their investigations. Some hypnotists had no advanced training in the specific techniques developed to facilitate accurate memories. Some had no formal training in psychology or the ethical use of hypnosis. The hypnosis sessions focused on the acquisition of information. Sometimes investigative hypnotists had no training in the therapeutic techniques that must be employed when there is underlying trauma. Sometimes frightening memories emerged, and the experiencer was left with increased anxiety. Those with latent psychiatric problems, lying just below the surface, descended into an acute episode after their hypnosis session. Professional hypnotherapists have intake forms that ask for their client's medical history. They have completed advanced courses and will not use you experimentally.

I have received a multitude of inquiries from experiencers who believe hypnosis is the royal pathway to the truth. There is a major problem with this idea: hypnosis cannot validate an abduction experience unless there are two or more witnesses, all of whom have amnesia for a specific event and all of whom have partial recall. Then each witness must be hypnotized separately by a hypnotist or independent hypnotists who do not ask leading questions. For example, if a hypnotist directs you to describe the room you have entered without first asking if your eyes are open, you can very easily confabulate a response, especially if you view the hypnotist as an authority figure. Amnesia must be reinstated at the end of each session and cannot be lifted until later when all witnesses have completed their hypnosis sessions. Otherwise, the witnesses' memories will be contaminated, and the evidence brought forth will be worthless.

The validity of an experience will increase if you, the experiencer, were traveling to a specific destination with an expected arrival time. Family members or friends might have been awaiting your arrival, but you did not appear at the appointed time. In fact, you arrived several hours later than anticipated and had no viable explanation for your tardiness. You possess a vague memory of seeing a bright light racing in your direction. Physical evidence, such as damaged clothing, physical injuries, radioactivity, and magnetic fields, can support the veracity of a missing time experience. New emotional trauma with no viable mundane explanation might suggest that something highly unusual has occurred. The great difficulty investigators face is this type of abduction has rarely occurred since the 1990s.

Does this mean that all abductions have ended? Of course not! They have only transformed. Today's experiencers are taken from their homes, usually at night when they are asleep, or even when they are wide awake. Some experiencers feel they are being taken out of body. Our newer experiencers are usually the offspring of an older generation of experiencers who were abducted while driving, hunting, fishing, camping, hiking, or playing on their family farm. Contact has become largely generational. Thousands of experiencers have described the same process. The same procedures are performed with the same medical equipment. The demeanor and job descriptions of the NHI entities are the same. Hypnotherapists and researchers hear it over and over again. We have come to believe that longitudinal, sociological, reproductive, and genetic studies are being carried out. We differ in opinion on the final outcome and the benevolence of the NHI entities who are carrying out this plan, but there is little difference in the actual process.

If you are a generational experiencer, your children might carry many of the gifts that you, your parents, or your grandparents acquired, such as increased intelligence and a high degree of empathy for others. You or your parents will probably have an increased level of intelligence, intuition or psychic ability, increased spirituality, a sense of universal connectedness, and a higher than average concern for the environment. You are probably empathic, meaning that you can sense the energy, emotions, or physical well-being of other people, even if they are not present. You will feel extremely uncomfortable in a large crowd, especially if mob behavior is being displayed. If you hurt someone, you will feel their pain as if it were your own.

If you or your family are empathic, if you sense a kind of tingling when you are in the presence of others like yourself, or if you hear certain tones when experiencers are nearby, you can rest assured that you are an experiencer as well. True experiencers are generally not greedy or self-centered. They look reflectively within and radiate kindness. They do not attempt to control or dominate others. They are good stewards to our planet and all that live here. This sense of universal connectedness makes xenophobia seem cruel and warlike behavior savage.

HOW TO INVESTIGATE YOUR EXPERIENCES

If you are still not certain that your abduction/contact suspicions are founded in reality, you've come to the right place. This chapter assists you with ideas on you how to investigate your own experiences. First, let's explore the best ways to document your evidence.

1. Keep a journal by your bedside. When you awaken with signs that indicate you have been outside your natural environment, document the date, time, and all of your memories. Do it immediately. If you wait, they might slip away.

2. Examine yourself in a mirror. Is your clothing in the same condition it was in before your event? Or is it inside out or backward? Do you recognize your clothing, or are you wearing something that belongs to someone else? Has it been torn or stained? If so, place your clothing in a brown paper bag and store it in a dark, warm closet for at least a month. Make a note on your calendar on the appointed day when you are to retrieve it from your closet. When your month is up, remove your clothing from the bag and inspect it. If something has been deposited on it, contact me. Photograph it, preferably indoors and without a flash. Then go into a dark room and examine it under a UV (black) light. If it fluoresces, photograph the fluorescence without a flash. Send a copy of your photo to me. If we believe that you have collected significant evidence that warrants scientific analysis, I will ask you to file an investigation report at *www.mufon.com*. Do not act impulsively

and send your evidence to MUFON Headquarters. MUFON has specific chain of custody protocols that must be followed.

3. Examine your body for evidence or ask for assistance from your spouse or significant other. Look for unusual marks that could not have a commonplace explanation, such as bug bites, blemishes, scratches, bumps, and bruises that happen to all of us. The ERT maintains a collection of photos that we have received from experiencers. Although we do not publish this information, we can compare your marks to others in our catalog. If they match, it will strengthen your evidence.

4. If you have not already done so, purchase a UV (black) light. You can find a variety of UV flashlights for sale on the Internet. They range in price from $5.99 to $40.00 or more. As an investigator, I invested in an expensive model. For personal use, you might wish to spend only a few dollars. If you believe that you have been taken physically, enter a dark room and inspect your body with your UV light. If you find fluorescence, photograph it under the UV light, in the dark, and without a flash. Be sure to photograph only areas of your body that are normally exposed at the beach. We do not want to see your genitals. In fact, yeast and bacteria in the genital region will fluoresce under a UV light. If this occurs, see your physician for treatment.

    A variety of common substances fluoresce under a UV light. They include pesticides, detergents, oils, and fungus. Our investigators know what to look for. One wannabe or hoaxer used a fluorescent felt-tip marker on her skin and filed an investigation report with MUFON. You can imagine her embarrassment when the investigator immediately recognized it as a fraud.

5. Committed UFO investigators have purchased the expensive equipment needed for a scientifically oriented forensic

investigation. A TriField Meter will measure magnetic, electromagnetic, and electric fields, plus radio-microwave frequency. The cost of a TriField Meter ranges from $135 for a used model, to $200 for a new one. Electromagnetic fields can be tricky to measure. A gaussmeter can measure only one field, so it might miss a different strong field even when one is present. The TriField Meter is superior because it is a three-axis measuring device that will measure the true strength of the field. It is always important to measure electromagnetic fields in the ambient environment prior to measuring fields associated with a possible contact event. Earth emits a magnetic field, which will be detectable. In addition to this, the electrical appliances in your home emit electromagnetic frequencies. The meter will always sound a buzzing tone when it is first turned on, as it adjusts to the natural environment. It will also detect geomagnetic storms caused by solar activity, electrical storms, and the electrical field on objects and in the human body. Your body might register a strong electrical field immediately following a contact event. If you decide to purchase a TriField Meter, you will need to experiment with it. You'll notice that the needle will jump and it will register a tone when you walk toward it. If it registers 1000 VPM at a distance of twelve feet from your body, this response is indicative that an NHI experience may have occurred.

It is common for experiencers to notice electromagnetic malfunctions after an event. Of the 550 participants in MUFON's Experiencer Survey, 57 percent stated that lights blinked out when they walked underneath them after a contact event, 46 percent reported computer malfunctions, and 27 percent said their appliances burned out. Some experiencers report time clock malfunctions at their place of employment, but only for themselves. Product scanners in stores might not register product prices when recent experiencers stand directly in front them. Appliances might turn on and off by themselves. A small percentage of experiencers cannot wear digital watches.

MUFON's Experiencer Survey discovered that some experiencers have electromagnetic malfunctions on a regular basis, whereas a smaller percentage of experiencers report major problems immediately after a contact event.

IMPLANTS

If you truly believe that you are an experiencer, you have probably searched for an implant that the NHI entities inserted into your body. If you discovered that you have one, you might be thinking about having it removed. Derrel Sims and the late Dr. Roger Leir specialized in the surgical removal of these highly unusual devices. A few have undergone scientific analysis in laboratories.

In the past, we believed that implants were tracking devices that the NHI entities used to find the people they wished to abduct. This idea has some merit because we know that an experiencer who, for example, lives in California can be abducted while on vacation in Europe. Experiencers believed that the removal of their implant would effectively end their abductions, so those who wanted their experiences to cease sought out implant removal. We now know that experiencers have fled their homes and relocated to other parts of the United States in an effort to escape their captors, but their abductions usually continued.

In the past, experiencers believed that the removal of their implant would make them invisible to their abductors. Today's evidence contradicts this idea. The majority of experiencers who underwent surgery to remove an implant have continued to be taken. And some who felt remorseful after the implant was removed were pleased when the visitations continued.

Old implants can be detected when a powerful magnet is placed over them. However, many believe that today's implants are biological and virtually impossible to detect in the human body. No visible insertion point can be located, and no surrounding scar tissue can be detected under a microscope.

Leir and Sims discovered that the implants they had removed have unusual properties. The tiny devices are coated with a tough material that resists attempts to puncture it. Implants had a second function: to create an environment that caused the human immune system to accept its presence. No inflammatory response was noted, so the human body did not reject them. A highly elevated level of proprioceptive nerve fibers were connected to the objects. This was a highly unusual finding. Dr. Leir stated that the implants often resisted removal and traveled away from the surgeon's scalpel, as if they had intelligence. Laboratory analyses discovered isotopic ratios of meteoric origin, not found on Earth, in the material that comprised the implants. Sometimes rare Earth minerals were noted. The implants appeared to have a crystalline structure using nano-technology far in advance of devices manufactured on our planet. One emitted a radio frequency that could transmit into deep space. To say the least, they are indeed interesting!

Currently, I am unaware of a medical doctor who devotes time to the removal and scientific analysis of implants. Dr. Leir's death left a gap in our effort to analyze these implants. Following Dr. Leir's death, a scientific team at MUFON developed protocols for the removal and analysis of what they call Anomalous Foreign Objects (AFO), not implants. However, experiencers will have to convince their own physicians to remove the foreign object and pay their own the medical expenses. MUFON does not have funding for these procedures.

If an experiencer wishes to have an AFO analyzed by a cooperating scientist, strict protocols must be followed. MUFON's Evidence

Review Board will be notified and provided with all evidence relative to the alleged AFO. Thereafter, the MUFON Evidence Review Board will assign the investigators they deem appropriate. They will conduct an investigation, ascertain that certain release forms are signed, and write interim and final reports. The AFO (implant) will become the property of MUFON and will not be returned to the experiencer.

My years of research and communication with experiencers have led me to conjecture that implants have at least four functions:

1. They might be tracking devices, as previously thought.
2. They might also be used as communication devices to facilitate telepathic exchanges between the experiencer and the nonhumans who placed them there.
3. They might be used to elevate the experiencer's vibrational frequency to expedite the process used when the human subject is transferred to an alien environment.
4. Perhaps they can detect health conditions within the human body.

CASE STUDY WITH EVIDENCE

We know that some experiencers have received healing from the NHI entities with whom they have established a relationship. Jim is an experiencer from Canada, whose case I have been investigating since 2012. On March 12, 2012, he filed an investigation report with MUFON, and I was asked to contact him. He reported a slow-moving, large, orange light that had come within 500–600 feet from his location and stopped for approximately fifteen seconds. It left the area in a skipping motion after he observed it for three and a half to four minutes. I filed his investigation report and thought that nothing more would come my way. However, he contacted me on January 29, 2013. This time he had awakened with a bloody Y-shaped wound on the top of his head. It was a fresh cut, and the blood had not dripped onto his pillowcase.

Five months later, Jim discovered what appeared to be a freshly healed incision on his groin, as if a lymph node had been removed. Only a month later, he awakened feeling drained of energy and in pain. Bilateral bruises developed on his upper arms, and he sensed that he had struggled to escape but had been held tightly by his NHI escorts.

In February 2014, he awakened at 4:30 a.m. and retrieved the morning edition of the newspaper. Feeling wide awake, he sat down to read the daily news. His next immediate memory was truly startling. As if only a moment had passed, he awoke trembling and perspiring profusely. When he gained his composure, he walked into his bathroom and discovered the presence of another Y-shaped mark on the crown of his head. Additionally, the T-shirt that he had been wearing was now on inside out and backward. He would never have put it on this way because it was uncomfortable on his neck. He vaguely recalled a commotion in his room and discovered that he had recorded fast clicks and chattering sounds on his cell phone and a photograph of a strange blue light. His household lights blinked out when he walked near them, and he seemed to be super charged with electricity.

Jim was bothered by an invisible entity that seemed to be walking on his bed whenever he laid down, whether it was during the day or at night. It had weight but seemingly no density, as he could not see it. I have since learned that 75 percent of MUFON's abductees (those with UFO Abduction Syndrome) and 65 percent of the experiencers who completed the Experiencer Survey reported the feeling that something unseen was walking on their bed. I had an identical experience many years ago at my mother's home.

Jim's experience with his T-shirt helped me write protocol #2 (mentioned on page 50) for the collection of evidence. It became part of an experiment to generate the growth of a pink powdery substance similar to the substance found on my aunt Betty Hill's dress. I hadn't informed him of this. Amazingly, two weeks later, he discovered a pink hue on his T-shirt. I was determined to send it to a scientist for analysis, so I asked him to send it to me. It arrived at my home in Florida, and I took it outside to photograph it, exposing it to ultraviolet light. I then forwarded it to the analytical chemist who had performed the scientific analysis of the substance on my aunt Betty's dress. The experiment failed, probably due to the shirt's exposure to the winter cold during transport and Florida's UV light. Almost none of the pink was visible when it arrived at the lab, and the residue that was left didn't match the residue on Betty's dress. The chemist found an abundance of perspiration. This alone confirms Jim's statement that he was perspiring profusely when he awoke. I blame myself for this failure, but I have learned from my mistake and have altered my protocol.

Within days of Jim's experience, which sounds more like an abduction than friendly contact, he discovered a new BB-size lump under the skin on his left arm, between his wrist and elbow, that moved when touched. I suspected that it would travel up his arm and disappear, as has occurred with other experiencers that I have worked with. Surprisingly, it remained in position. Jim made the decision to request surgical removal of the object by his physician, and I arranged for its scientific analysis following MUFON's protocols. The tiny metallic sphere was surgically removed and placed in Jim's bodily fluid, as recommended by Dr. Leir, in an attempt to prevent it from self-destructing. It was carefully wrapped in Styrofoam and dry ice for safe transport. Jim securely packaged it for shipping, and we eagerly awaited the scientific report. All MUFON chain-of-custody procedures were followed.

We were terribly disappointed, and Jim was extremely angry, when we were informed that the sphere was not in the package when it arrived at the scientific laboratory. He had developed an infection that sent him to the hospital. And for what? I experienced a feeling of helplessness and frustration. What had occurred? We had followed all of the protocols. Had someone stolen it? Had the US Postal Service opened it? It had not been tampered with when it arrived at MUFON Headquarters. The scientist not only photographed the package but also assured us that it was tightly wrapped when it arrived at the laboratory, exactly as it had been when it left Canada. Were implants now self-destructing in bodily fluid? A couple of weeks later, I received a frantic message from a state director. She asked MUFON to waive its protocols, as the tiny sphere that had been surgically removed from another experiencer was dissolving before her eyes! It appears that the nonhumans who inserted the implant do not want it to fall into the custody of human scientists.

In early 2014, Jim conveyed some troubling news to me. The lymph nodes on the left side of his neck were greatly enlarged and wrapping around the side of his neck to the back. He was scheduled for a presurgery head and neck conference at Manitoba Cancer Care in March 2014. His diagnosis was lymphoma. This was very distressing news indeed! I asked him to request healing from his NHI visitors, and I would do the same. It was a long shot, but anything would be better than nothing at this point in time.

Jim had been photographing lighted orbs that he'd seen floating in his home, but prior to his surgery, he mailed an astonishing video to me. It showed a beautiful white orb surrounded by a light blue halo. The orb slid down the wall next to his bedroom closet and then changed direction. It flew like a butterfly, morphing as it crossed his bedroom and hovered over his body, shooting rainbow light beams downward. It then dove into his body.

The following day, the nodes on Jim's neck had significantly decreased in size. On the day of his surgery, four small necrotic nodes

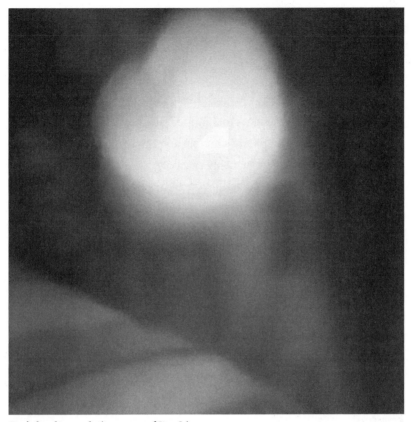

Jim's healing orb *(courtesy of Jim S.)*

were removed. No cancer was noted. It seems like a miracle! But our NHI visitors are known for healing their own contacts. Thirty-nine percent of the abductees in MUFON's Experiencer Survey stated that they had been healed by NHI entities.

Jim presented excellent, clear photographic video of the moving orb that confirmed his testimony and a medical record from the oncology department at his surgical care facility. Point-and-shoot photos of something unseen are worthless as evidence. I have viewed hundreds of video frames and still shots sent to me that show nothing of significance. Pareidolia, the human tendency to see faces (ETs) or familiar images (UFOs) where none exist, is a human trait. We must be very careful when it comes to photographic evidence.

HYPNOSIS

Now let's discuss hypnosis, which appears to have fallen out of favor in recent years. In the past, information retrieved through forensic hypnosis was admissible as evidence in a court of law. Forensic hypnosis gained notoriety in 1976, when the story of a school bus driver and twenty-seven students in California was publicized in the media. Criminals had kidnapped and buried them and were holding them for ransom. Luckily, the bus driver escaped from what would have been his untimely grave and led the police back to rescue the students. The perpetrators were eventually captured and successfully prosecuted, but only after the bus driver had submitted to forensic hypnosis. Hypnosis facilitated the accurate recall of the license plate on the kidnappers' van.

This account is only one of many examples in which hypnosis has been used successfully to recall accurate, detailed information. The problem with hypnosis lies in the information that the bus driver might have falsely recalled if he had no biographical memory of observing the license plate but felt pressured to remember. False recall will occur when a police officer offers two license plate numbers and asks a witness to choose between the two. This is a clear example of leading the witness and implanting a false memory. Once remembered in hypnosis, the false memory will seem as real as real. This is an example of why hypnosis fell into disfavor during the 1980s, when "false memory syndrome" advocates pointed out the propensity toward confabulation when no real memory exists.

However, the inaccurate recall of certain details is a characteristic of recall in general. We remember the events that are most significant to us and forget those we identify as trivial. If a memory is so disturbing that it cannot be successfully integrated into our consciousness, we might undergo the adaptive process of repression or distortion. Some of the detailed information in recovered traumatic memories may have shape-shifted over time, approximating the real experience but differing somewhat from it. However, memories of a traumatic experience might remain fresh in a person's mind and replay over and over again. These memories can remain vivid and clear. Simply stated, conscious recall and hypnotic regression display similar characteristics. They are more of an adaptive process than an accurate video recording.

We must be mindful that since hypnosis involves human subjects, by its very nature, it can never guarantee absolute certainty. However, techniques can be employed to reduce the possibility of confabulation and increase the chances for a true regression. The hypnotist must be sensitive to the fact that hypnosis can profoundly affect the subject's subsequent memory and emotional well-being. For this reason, it is extremely important that the experiencer's emotional well-being takes precedence over the desire to collect information.

When memories are recalled through hypnosis, the individual and the trained therapist must rely on their own knowledge and experience to determine the reality of the recall. Is there evidence? Were there witnesses? Was information recalled consistent with memories produced by other experiencers? Has this information been concealed from the public and not given to the experiencer? It is dishonest and unethical for a hypnotist to prepare an experiencer by saying, "You might remember this or you might find yourself undergoing this procedure." This is one reason that hypnosis should be conducted by qualified therapists, without an agenda, who have undergone specialized training for their work with experiencers that will reduce the possibility of producing false memories.

In 1984, UFO abduction investigators in New York came under pressure for allegedly using questionable practices in the treatment and care of suspected UFO abductees. They were accused of offering treatment to persons who had been traumatized by unknown means and were treating these individuals without the proper credentials required to successfully carry out this therapeutic process. The hypnotists were accused of surreptitiously employing procedures that the authorities thought were detrimental to the well-being and health of the abductees.

The state issued a cease-and-desist order to the hypnotists, whom they identified as practicing the unethical treatment of alleged UFO abductees. The reason stated was that the hypnotists were undereducated and undercredentialed. They were UFO investigators who employed hypnosis to recover abduction memories but fell short in their knowledge of psychology and the damaging impact that recovered memories, especially if they are traumatic, can have on people.

This was the time frame in which I commenced my study of hypnosis and the academic research studies pertaining to its characteristics. My findings propelled me to become an advocate for the ethical use of hypnosis with experiencers. As mentioned earlier, some early abduction investigators used hypnosis improperly and without sensitivity to the traumatic emotional impact that disturbing recovered memories can generate.

Although skeptics have insisted that "false memory syndrome" is a primary cause of abduction memories, an academic study of 236 adults at University College, London, revealed that many recovered memories are true. Dr. Bernice Andrews, the research scientist who conducted the study stated, "There is increasing evidence that many recovered memories cannot be explained by so-called False Memory Syndrome. A substantial portion of these memories have been corroborated."[1] The key to the accurate recovery of repressed traumatic memories seems to lie in methodology. When hypnotized persons are remembering an event as if they were there reliving it, and no suggestive techniques have been employed by the hypnotherapist, accurate recall is at its highest level.

Some experiencers have suffered anxiety after unqualified, undereducated hypnotists allowed them to retain recall of a painful or frightening memory. Well-trained hypnotherapists will never instill a fear reaction in their clients. Techniques are used that provide an emotionally safe environment for their clients. Skilled hypnotherapists can reinstate amnesia, to enable the repressed memory to remain in the subconscious mind until the experiencer and hypnotherapist can safely work through it, without inducing traumatic memories. Although amnesia sometimes occurs spontaneously, it can also be initiated as a direct or indirect hypnotic suggestion.

Whereas traditional hypnosis is a safe procedure for most people, for some individuals, hypnotic regression may not be advisable. For your own protection, a certified hypnotist/hypnotherapist or a licensed mental health provider who uses therapeutic hypnosis will determine whether your unique medical or psychological history suggests any factors that may preclude you from proceeding with hypnosis. If you have a psychological disorder that you are coping with effectively, and you undergo hypnosis to uncover your abduction memories, the procedure could exacerbate your problem and bring it to the surface. Be honest with yourself and your hypnotist. Your emotional well-being is of utmost importance.[2]

When trauma is evident, therapy by a licensed mental health practitioner is essential. Certified hypnotherapists are not always licensed mental health practitioners. Be certain that your therapist has a minimum of a master's degree in counseling if you are suffering from trauma. Emotional pain can be addressed by a licensed psychotherapist who specializes in the treatment of trauma. Eye movement desensitization and reprocessing, or EDMR, therapy is particularly successful for the reduction of traumatic stress through the use of desensitizing techniques.

When I was young and had a possible abduction experience, my hypnosis was facilitated by a doctor, whom I assumed was a psychologist. I later learned that he was a UFO and abduction researcher with a PhD in an unrelated field. My frightening memories of being transported to the craft in some type of beam were disturbing, so he ended my session as soon as I began to experience terror. This memory led to increased anxiety. When I voiced my feelings of distress and fear to him, he could not help me. He did not offer support to those he hypnotized. He only wanted to learn more about my events. This new, frightening knowledge persisted for several years until I underwent hypnosis of a different kind with a gentle, compassionate hypnotist who knew that she should never leave a person in a fearful state. She moved me past being transported to the craft to memories of kind, compassionate treatment. I will forever be grateful to her.

In my role as an experiencer advocate, I have watched for fraudulent hypnotherapists with a vigilant eye. One of these was passing herself off as a regression therapist, but in reality, she was a high school dropout. I counseled her on the consequences of misrepresentation and urged her to cease and desist. This individual closed her practice to experiencers and worked only on weight loss and smoking cessation. It is extremely important for the experiencer population to receive the services they are paying for and not be treated by an undereducated, unethical charlatan.

I am strongly opposed to hypnotic regression via the telephone, Skype, Facebook Messenger, or other online video-conferencing sites. Why? Barney Hill rose from his seat and attempted to flee when Dr. Simon forced him to remember his terrifying abduction. Think about what might have occurred if he had been speaking to Dr. Simon via the telephone. In his safe Boston office, Dr. Simon took physical control of Barney. He gave a firm command and physically touched him. Barney had run toward the window in Dr. Simon's office. Imagine the liability issues if he had plunged two to three stories onto the pavement below.

What would you do if you were miles away from your hypnotist or hypnotherapist and your connection was lost during a critical period? You would eventually emerge from hypnosis, but you would retain the level of fear you experienced even though your emotional response might have awakened you. Your fearful memories would remain unresolved. The National Guild of Hypnotists clearly states that it is unethical to perform distance regression hypnosis.

With regard to memory retrieval, be cautious. Although you may recall accurate information under hypnosis, if the hypnotherapist asks leading questions, you might confabulate or create false memories based on what you have heard, read, or watched. Your hypnotherapist will ask a leading question to test your propensity for creating false memories and can use methodology to minimize confabulation. Ask about this before your hypnosis session.

Certified hypnotherapists can employ other healing techniques when your level of trauma does not require the services of a psychotherapist. One successful technique was developed by Dolores Cannon (1931–2014), a past life regression therapist. She developed the Quantum Healing Hypnosis Technique (QHHT), a unique hypnosis method that promotes emotional healing. Although it is not effective for everyone, it has been a godsend to many.

Her QHHT hypnosis taps into the Subconscious mind (with a capital S, not to be confused with the subconscious mind referred to by psychologists). The Subconscious has also been referred to at the higher self, the soul, and source consciousness. Her method takes clients into the deepest trance possible. She called it a state of somnambulism, which she defined as being the same as the minutes that precede and follow sleep.

The QHHT method elicits only the information that will be helpful and healing to the individual. It is focused on healing and is believed to provide instant healing to many. Every lifetime is relived as if it were in the here and now. Everything exists in the now and is available for quantum healing.

In the book *The Keepers of the Garden* (1993), she introduced information pertaining to the extraterrestrial origins of humankind. She wrote that a council planted our seed on this planet and oversees our development. She introduced the idea that time is not linear, and we can exist in other lives and locations simultaneously. Human thought creates our reality, and negative human consciousness generated through the global media, which focuses on war, violence, destruction, drug abuse, and greed, perpetuates the negative. Today's consciousness studies are an outgrowth and expansion of these ideas. Nonhuman entities have independently provided nearly identical information to me even though I had not read her books or studied her techniques at the time I received it.

Dolores Cannon's journey into ET contact began through her association with MUFON. At a MUFON meeting, she was introduced to a woman who believed she had been abducted by extraterrestrials. Through her work with experiencers, Cannon learned that some people have been visited since they were young children, by extraterrestrial races, who have had a multigenerational association with some families. She learned that UFO abductions are actually not abductions at all. They are mutually agreed upon contact experiences, made prior to one's incarnation on Earth, to offer assistance to one another. She believed that our negative perspective has been shaped by the media, which focuses on fear and loathing. Many of today's experiencers have come to Earth to assist in the development of humankind and to elevate human consciousness, increase spirituality, and lift our vibrational frequency to a higher level. If we can accomplish this, life on our planet will become easier and less chaotic.

You have probably surmised the difference between investigating your abduction/contact experiences and engaging in healing therapy. They do not have to be mutually exclusive. Some therapeutic hypnotists can accomplish both goals, whereas other methodologies focus on one or the other.

If you are seeking emotional healing and do not have deep-seated trauma that requires treatment by a mental health professional, you might find QHHT hypnosis worthy of exploration. I was so impressed by QHHT that I studied Dolores Cannon's technique and am now a QHHT Level 2 practitioner. You'll find a list of QHHT therapists on Cannon's website at *https://dolorescannon.com*.

Regardless of the type of hypnosis you select, I recommend having a support system in place. Do not try to brave your situation alone. Some experiencers have a strong, supportive family that they can depend on for emotional support. Others do not. If you find yourself alone with your memories, look for a professionally run or experiencer-facilitated self-help support group. Although they are few and far between, online support groups fill the gap. MUFON's ERT can help you locate one. As additional evidence is collected and investigators realize that contact is real, an increasing number of MUFON chapters are hosting meetings and workshops for experiencers. Additionally, some UFO conferences host workshops or support groups for experiencers. The simple act of sharing your story with a nonjudgmental person in a supportive environment can lift years of weight off your shoulders.

The next chapter will assist you with the stages that experiencers go through during their journey from denial to acceptance.

CHAPTER 3 CHECKLIST: TOOLS AND IDEAS

Use this checklist to assist you in your effort to determine what is occurring in your life. It also offers reminders in case you make the decision to undergo hypnosis.

Equipment for Your Own Investigation

- Journal and pen by your bedside
- Camera
- UV (black light) flashlight
- Electromagnetic field detector or TriField Meter
- Magnet
- Human body chart printed from the Internet
- Measuring tape
- Surveillance camera or infrared game camera if desired

Reminders Regarding Hypnosis

- The hypnotist and you should be in the same physical location during your sessions.
- Your hypnosis sessions should be carried out by an unbiased clinical hypnotherapist or certified hypnotist who has specialized training in working with abduction experiencers.
- Your hypnotist should be knowledgeable about experimental research findings regarding hypnosis, false memory formation, and the complexities of the human psychological experience.
- An ethical hypnotist will ask for your medical, social, and psychiatric history prior to your first hypnosis session.
- Send your investigation reports or your personal account of your UFO experience to your hypnotist to review prior to your first hypnosis session.

- Each session should be videotaped or audiotaped.
- If your investigator is at your session, this person should not ask you questions. A trained forensic hypnotist can elicit your memories without asking direct or leading questions.
- In the case of multiple witness abduction, all individuals should be hypnotized separately and posthypnotic amnesia should be induced at the end of each session.
- If you are working with a licensed hypnotherapist/psychotherapist, a posthypnotic suggestion for amnesia can be imposed at the end of each hypnosis session until you have recalled your amnestic memories and any intense emotions have been released. It will be a therapeutic process allowing for the assimilation and reintegration of information into your conscious memory. This approach can vary depending on the psychotherapist.
- Your hypnotherapist should facilitate your acceptance of the event through desensitization techniques, moving you from the role of victim to survivor. Consider having EMDR therapy with a licensed psychotherapist if you have PTSD.
- If you are seeing a certified hypnotist, posthypnotic suggestions and scripts to remove fears and phobias can be applied, along with the suggestion for self-hypnosis to reinforce the posthypnotic suggestions.
- The Quantum Healing Hypnosis Technique (QHHT) can be very therapeutic, but it should not be used as part of an investigation of your experiences. It might be more important than an investigation of your specific memories of abduction.
- Your psychological well-being should always be the first and foremost priority.
- Because of the serial nature of abduction, you will probably benefit from participation in a support group.

Chapter 4

THIS IS MY REALITY: WHAT NOW?

Ann Castle

Imagine this: after a long day you put on the blue pajamas your mother gave you for your last birthday, and you snuggle into your comfortable bed. As you fall into a deep sleep, all is right in your world. Suddenly, something wakes you. You see terrifying figures around your bed. You try to scream but cannot move.

The next thing you know, you wake up, freezing, outside in the back yard. It is dawn and the birds are starting to chirp. Your blue pajamas are gone, and you are wearing a strange pink nightgown streaked with dirt. You stagger to your feet and realize you have had a horrifying and bizarre experience.

You try to convince yourself the entire thing was a dream, or maybe you were sleepwalking, but you *are* wearing a stranger's clothes! Your mind searches for a logical explanation. However, there is a fleeting *moment* when you realize that *beings from another world* have taken you, and that moment is more terrifying than anything you have experienced in your life. Worse still, a part of you knows it really happened. What now?

In *that moment* you are too traumatized to realize that your life will never be the same again, that your view of what you can trust and believe and what is real in the universe will forever change. In

that moment you have unknowingly jumped on an emotional, social, and intellectual roller-coaster ride that may whip you around
for years before you recalibrate to a new comfort level of how the
world works. You will never again regard the world, the universe,
the government, the military, politics, science, science fiction, consciousness, religion, medicine, psychiatry, outer space, society, conspiracy theories, the headline news—or even your own family—in
quite the same way again.

You will now have secrets: secret experiences and secret memories. You may feel as if much of what you believed was a lie, and now
you don't know what to believe. You don't yet know that from *that
moment* forward you will forever think of your life in two parts—
before and after—*that moment*, when everything changed.

This chapter walks you through common stages experiencers
go through once they realize (or strongly suspect) they have had a
real experience with nonhuman intelligence or nonhuman intelligent entities, or an experience with paranormal forces, or both. The
journey through these stages varies with each experiencer. You will
go through some stages simultaneously and repeat them several
times. You may feel as if you are working your way up a spiral and
hitting the same stage multiple times as you go up, but each time
you encounter that stage it is easier.

Depending on your specific experience, you may be traumatized,
excited, thrilled, terrified, numb, angry, paralyzed, vindicated (you
always knew there were aliens), happy, horrified, peaceful, blessed,
or exhilarated, and you may feel many of these emotions at once.
Therefore, the amount of time you spend moving through these
stages will vary, depending on the kind of experience you had, your
positive or negative perception of it, and what you believe may have
happened.

Ultimately, the goal of this chapter is to help you understand the
emotions you will have as you integrate your experience into your

new life, for it will be a new life with broadened views about the nature of reality and your role in it. As you go through these stages, you will ultimately create a new worldview (about how science, military, governments, society, and the world operate) and a new belief system (the cornerstones of your moral code, religion, spirituality, and the ground rules for how you live your life and think about the universe). You will experience new realizations about yourself and the universe—perhaps an enhanced and deeply satisfying spirituality and happiness, and perhaps ultimately a recalibration of yourself into a happier, wiser, and better human being. A questionnaire at the end of this chapter helps you determine what stage you are in and can act as a guidepost through your journey.

There are four common stages in this journey commonly experienced in this order:

1. Shock and Denial
2. Fear and Anger
3. Exploration and Isolation
4. Relinquishment and Recalibration

SHOCK AND DENIAL

Shock: The first stage is utter shock. It is one thing to intellectualize about the possibility of NHI or the paranormal, but a whole other thing to experience it. During this stage you will be very distracted in your work and home life. You may or may not be able to share your experience with loved ones. You will keep replaying the event in your mind and may feel you are inside a bad movie that no else is watching.

You will grope for logical explanations of your event and have a mixed reaction to this effort. On one hand, you want to be wrong about what happened so your world can stay the same and you don't have to change anything. No one likes to change. On the other hand, if you are wrong about what happened, how can you trust your own perceptions, and how can you cope with the madness of reality? Plus, if you were wrong about what happened, then what exactly *did* happen? You may feel detached, and going about your life normally will be hard, because you are trying to act normal after an abnormal event!

When you are in shock, you want normality. You may turn to your psychological crutches, such as overeating, oversleeping, alcohol, marijuana, too much television/sex/partying/online gaming/shopping/jogging/working/whatever. You may isolate yourself in your bedroom or be terrified of being alone. You will already be feeling the effects of the next stage, *Fear and Anger*.

If symptoms of shock interfere with your normal life, cause you great distress, or last longer than a month or so, you may also have post-traumatic stress disorder. PTSD can manifest soon after any trauma, or years later. It can come and go for many years. You may be unable to get memories out of your mind, unable to sleep, or you may be hyper alert to any stimuli, such as loud noises. You may feel the need to obtain a weapon and keep it near your bed, but if you do, please consider other family members, especially children, who could be harmed by weapons. Refer to Chapter 10 for easier and safer ways to thwart abductions.

If you think you have PTSD, or if your symptoms are so severe you cannot function well, please consider going to counseling and/or seeing a qualified medical provider who may be able to prescribe medication for you. A support group for experiencers could also help you, but if none exist in your area, you may want to start one. The sharing and comradery that occur in these groups offer tremendous help and solace to new experiencers. Simply being able to discuss your experience can be very healing, and you may make friends who accept and understand what you have been through.

NHI entity by bed *(courtesy of Chad W., ERT)*

Give yourself time to adjust. Be patient. You have gone through a trauma, and your mind is struggling to deal with it. You can find constructive ways of comforting yourself that increase the positive-feeling endorphins in your brain by exercising or enjoying activities with friends and family. Remind yourself that your life still has many normal aspects to it, and they are not likely to change. Life goes on, and you will too!

Denial: As you work through your shock and grope for logical explanations—but find none—you will likely try to deny what happened to you. Denial is a common reaction to any trauma. Denial is a protective reaction of the mind that enables you to ignore a trauma in order to focus on more immediate necessities, such as holding down your job.

When you hold onto denial too long, you are subconsciously using a large amount of emotional and mental energy to repress the experience, which saps your energy. Denial is also a form of procrastination and inaction, where you choose to live in a fantasy rather than face what happened to you. Here are some signs you may be in denial for too long:

- Since your event, you are tired all the time. Maybe your mind and body are using a lot of energy to keep your trauma repressed.
- Fragmented memories of the traumatic experience intrude into your mind. You cannot repress the memories forever, so they leak out and disturb your peace or dreams.
- A movie scene or other reminder similar to your experience suddenly overwhelms you with memories about your event. This is quite common with NHI experiences. For example, one experiencer remembered playing with small clowns in her backyard when she was a child as an ice cream truck drove by playing *Twinkle Twinkle Little Star*. Twenty years later she heard the song again and realized with horror the clowns were really Grey NHI entities.

Here are some tips to help you overcome denial:

- **Accept that you are in denial.** You can't overcome a problem if you deny it exists, and being in denial about being in denial is an obvious, circuitous trap. Be honest and gentle with yourself.

- **Consider the evidence.** Remind yourself of the event and the objective evidence, such as missing time, marks on your body, or the strange dreams you have never had before. *Trust your gut: your intuition is a powerful tool, and your gut never lies to you.*

- **Consider alternative reactions and ideas.** Even though you are trying to maintain your old belief systems about reality, start broadening your mind with *what if* ideas: What if the experience did happen? How does that change you or your world? One point of this exercise is to open your mind to possibilities that may provide answers to your dilemma. Eventually, these ideas will help wear down your denial. Another reason for this exercise is that in almost all *what if* scenarios you can imagine, you still survive: this helps convince you that your life will indeed go on, which also helps break down denial.

Without denial, we are happier, are more effective, and have more energy, so the sooner you get through this stage, the better. More importantly, when we conquer our denial, we take back our power from the situation, which is a psychologically stronger place to be. When you realize your experience was a real thing, you will move primarily into the stage of *Fear and Anger.*

FEAR AND ANGER

The second stage of the journey is fear and anger. With shock and denial, you are a confused victim who does not understand the reality of the situation. With fear and anger, you may be terrified and furious, but at least now you understand that something bizarre and real has occurred. Plus, you can be motivated by fear and empowered by anger to begin taking control of how you respond to your experience.

Fear: Fear is built into our DNA, our bodies, and our intuition. Without fear, we would die young, so you may want to *thank* your fear for often keeping you safe! It is natural for the bravest of people to be afraid of NHI entities because you have never anticipated them before, nor been trained in how to handle them. Some ufologists have considered that humans may be neurologically programmed to fear NHI entities, which makes us easier to control. There are two main things many experiencers fear: loss of control and fear of the unknown.

Loss of control: NHI entities took you without your permission, and you don't know if they will come back. You have no control over this situation, but you have learned to live with many other situations in which you also have no control, such as bad drivers on the road, severe weather, crime, accidents, financial setbacks, major illnesses, and even death. Usually, we are not burdened in our everyday lives thinking about these things, and eventually—perhaps in the recalibration stage—you will regard your NHI experience in the same way. You may also realize that the NHI entities brought you back relatively unharmed and will probably do so again.

Fear of the unknown: Once you realize your event was real, you may fear the unknown. You may have little memory of what happened, and you assume the worst. You don't know the intent or agenda of the NHI entities. The best way to overcome this fear is to become more educated on the topic, and reading this book is an excellent start! *The more you know, the more empowered you are!*

Ways to Overcome Fear

- Begin a meditation practice. There are many books and courses on mediation. It helps people feel stronger and more peaceful. Meditating for even five or ten minutes a day offers numerous health and psychological benefits. Refer to Chapter 10 for more information.
- Build your confidence by strengthening your body. Exercise more; practice weight training or martial arts. Eat well.
- Remind yourself of the times in your life you feared something needlessly. There will be many examples if you are honest with yourself.
- Find practical ways to address specific fears, such as sleeping with a nightlight if you are afraid of sleeping in the dark. If the experience happened on a certain road, try avoiding the road for a while or go there with a friend. Train yourself to be mindful of the clock should another event occur. This will help you determine if you have had missing time should another strange event occur.
- Spend more time with friends and loved ones. You don't have to confide your experience to them, but simply being with them more will help you realize that life goes on, and most of it is pretty normal.

Anger: Mixed with the fear, you will naturally be angry and indignant about your experience and its aftermath. You were living your life, minding your own business when this experience turned your world upside down. You will be angry at the NHI entities because you were kidnapped, violated, physically abused, and had your life interrupted. They may have inflicted physical pain upon you and left scars, marks, bleeding, or even injuries. They violated what you believe are your human rights, and you have no recourse for this injustice. You will be angry because now you are dealing with fear and its related angst, and you feel totally alone.

You may literally be angry at the world because your religion, the government, the military, academia, society, all authorities, science, your family, and the world in general—everyone who has given you your beliefs and taught you how to think—have lied to you about what is real! By now you realize that authorities know about NHI entities and are not telling us. How dare they keep this secret! You may feel betrayed by society because you were never taught how to deal with this reality. You know that people who report UFO sightings or encounters with NHI entities are ridiculed into silence or even lose their jobs for speaking the truth. You will be angry at the injustice.

You will be angry because you have no context for how to *think* about NHI entities, your experience, or how to work through it. You may also be angry because through no fault of your own you are left alone, adrift in unknown territory and unable to confide the most important experience of your life to anyone. You may even be angry at God for allowing your experience and for not protecting you because you are a good person who deserves better. This is a lot of anger to hold onto! Plus there are very few ways to express that anger because you can't readily talk about what happened to you!

The great tragedy, however, is not that you are very angry. The tragedy is what that anger is doing to you if you allow it to continue. We've all known angry people, and few of us want to be around them. Few emotions are more poisonous than anger, which creates bitterness, ruins your enjoyment of life, and if turned inward, causes depression. Others avoid angry people because they can feel the angry energy even if it is not expressed. Here are tips on overcoming anger:

- **Decide to let it go.** In many instances in life we are angry and there is no good solution or recourse to our problem: this is one of them. Admit you are angry and make a conscious decision to let go of your anger because it hurts *you* the most. No one else cares that you're angry! If letting go of it is very difficult, there may be an underlying reason why you are choosing to hold onto your anger. Perhaps holding onto it makes you "right" and you would rather be right than happy. Perhaps holding onto anger is a good excuse for not achieving things in your life because you are "wounded." Perhaps you fear that if you let go of anger, it means you are weak, but any spiritual leader, psychologist, or anyone in martial arts will tell you that letting go of anger makes you stronger.
- **Try the psychic cord-release technique.** Imagine the person or thing making you angry, and imagine a cord is attached to that person or thing and your navel. Imagine you are jerking the cord back from them, releasing yourself from their grip, and claiming back your power with every jerk of the cord. Perform this technique multiple times, and your anger will lessen.
- **Try the neurofeedback technique.** Close your eyes and imagine your anger. Encircle your dominant wrist with your other hand and squeeze it. As you squeeze it, exhale, release your anger, and release your wrist. Perform this technique multiple times, and your anger will lessen. This is good for any negative feeling.
- **Forgive the NHI.** Again, in many instances in life we are angry and don't understand the larger picture or the purpose of something. You can make a conscious decision to forgive someone or a situation, which is often easier if you are spiritually inclined. Forgiveness can work wonders in creating

inner peace. Anger can prevent forgiveness, so you may need to work on the anger first.

- **Educate yourself.** Learn about UFOs, NHI entities, and what other experiencers have gone through. Often the more knowledge you have, the smaller your emotional reaction is to it. On this journey you will eventually want some answers to your experience, and you will start exploring these topics, which is the beginning of the *Exploration and Isolation* stage.

EXPLORATION AND ISOLATION

Congratulations! You have made it through the worst stages of coming to grips with your new reality. It gets easier now, and parts of it are even entertaining! The pain of shock, denial, fear, and anger lessen a great deal, and with newfound knowledge you arrive at an even more powerful place psychologically. In the *Exploration and Isolation* stage you start to understand your experience better, grow as a person, and form your new worldview. This is a longer stage than the previous stages and will sometimes overlap all the stages. This stage may last months or years! This is an exciting stage as you explore new ideas, learn fascinating things, broaden your worldview, and possibly make friends with UFO enthusiasts and/ or fellow experiencers. Your network grows, your mind grows, your spirit grows, and you can become a better, stronger, more informed, and wiser person than you ever thought possible.

Exploration: Typically experiencers turn to the Internet and explore many websites. They buy books and lose themselves in the fascinating history of UFOs, experiencers, and their cover-ups. They may join MUFON to gain access to a terrific newsletter and other benefits, and they may join an experiencer support group or even start one. If you start one, you will be amazed at how many people in your locale may be experiencers. It is recommended that you screen attendees to make sure they would be a positive addition to your group. Some groups use Meetup.com to start.

Researching UFO and experiencer topics can be challenging and fascinating! However, because anyone can publish anything on the Internet, it is difficult to know whether the information you find is fact, opinion, or fabrication. The UFO field is filled with misinformation and disinformation purposely planted by governments and skeptics to distort the truth about NHI, UFOs, and the experiencer phenomena. Many videos are faked by people seeking attention or fame. You will probably not find reliable articles in mainstream media or on scientific or academic websites unless they are debunking the topics.

Some people claim to know the complete and absolute truth about UFOs, NHI entities, and their intent, but many of these people proselytize their own beliefs according to their religious or philosophical backgrounds. They wrap their own beliefs around a phenomenon and call it fact, even though they have no evidence.

In this stage you will learn facts that will later form new beliefs about the universe. You may learn that our galaxy is fairly young and that the universe is so vast that we can't find its edges. Even if one in a million stars had planets that could support intelligent life, there could still be billions of planets with intelligent life! As you explore, you will notice that there is much evidence to theorize that races of NHI have interacted with humans and this planet in the past and are continuing to do so. In other words, NHI entities have always been here and may have seeded this relatively young planet. (Refer to Appendix A, "Suggested Websites," and Appendix B, "Suggested Readings.")

Isolation: As you explore, you might be overwhelmed by information and may feel as if you have fallen down a rabbit hole. You may feel alienated (no pun intended) from family and friends, and so overwhelmed with information that you believe no one could understand what you are going through. This feeling is normal and indicates only that your mind and belief systems are stretching and considering broader possibilities about reality. As you sort through the information, you may seek some isolation as you examine how this knowledge impacts you. Indulge in some time alone to think about what you have learned. You are creating new beliefs as you adjust to this new reality, but don't forget that your family and friends still need you. Don't neglect people and responsibilities in your life. It is important to find balance between your normal life and your research.

RELINQUISHMENT AND RECALIBRATION

The final and longest stage of building your new worldview and belief system, *Relinquishment and Recalibration,* is the most intriguing. This stage will likely go on for years and include periodic visits to previous stages as you sort out more troubling questions. You may relinquish some beliefs, adopt new ones, and still be muddy about others; no one has all the answers. You will learn to live with doubt, unanswered questions, and ambiguity, but as uncomfortable as these can be, learning to live with them is a sign of psychological and spiritual maturity. As you learn to see existential puzzles as gray instead of black and white, you will broaden your mind, which will in turn provide you with some answers, knowledge, and more wisdom.

Relinquishment: We have all relinquished beliefs and ideas about our worldview or belief system in our lives before, as experience, facts, or maturity have made some older ideas obsolete. In other words, we grow up. For example, many young children believe in Santa Claus, but few teenagers do because their life experience, exposure to facts, and more mature analytical skills have proven to them that Santa Claus is a mythical being. The time when children realize that Santa Claus is a myth can be traumatic and sad: it can diminish childhood innocence as well as some Christmas joy and magic that are never regained.

However, as children mature, they can transform some of that lost joy and magic into a holiday spirit of generosity, which brings them greater happiness than the belief in Santa Claus did. Mature teenagers and adults may volunteer in soup kitchens, spend time with the elderly, or approach Christmas from a spiritual perspective. These experiences enrich them with joy and lasting memories in ways that toys from a mythical being could not. Often as people mature and shed old beliefs or ideas that no longer serve them, they discover a new and richer dimension of ideas that bring more value to their lives and spirits.

Just as a belief in Santa Claus no longer serves you, a belief in a limited universe, in which Earth is the only planet that contains intelligent life, also no longer serves your intellect or your psychological or spiritual maturity. In this stage you will relinquish many beliefs about

- Conspiracy theories—maybe some of them are right after all;
- How science is funded and why scientists find it difficult to change facts or theories;
- How the military and government conspire to keep us ignorant about UFOs and NHI entities;
- How the military-industrial complex influences politics, governments, and economies;
- How ancient the UFO and NHI phenomena are;
- How and why disclosure may happen, as well as barriers to disclosure;
- How alien technology may influence the future world;

- How acknowledgment of NHI entities may change religious or spiritual beliefs, Earth societies, and economies.

These are just a few topics that you will explore once you jump down the experiencer rabbit hole. You may temporarily fall back into anger and fear as you explore, but each time you relinquish an incorrect belief, you will be empowering yourself with greater knowledge, which in turn leads to wisdom.

Recalibration: This is the last stage of your journey and the most rewarding. Your shock and denial, fear and anger, are mostly gone. Recalibration is the longest stage and may last for years. In this stage you will make changes to your thinking, belief system, and worldview: you will simultaneously rectify some old beliefs and values, and integrate the old and the new into a worldview that reflects your new knowledge, wisdom, social maturity, and spiritual maturity. You will be making recalibrations to this worldview for the rest of your life as you encounter new information about UFOs and NHI.

You may find that your core beliefs about how the universe works no longer fit those of your family or social circle. Relationships may change, and you may seek out others with beliefs that align with yours. These are healthy reactions to rapid personal growth, and you will ultimately be a happier and wiser person because of it. Several areas of your life may recalibrate:

- Socially, you may be more accepting of different people, their cultures, and their beliefs because you realize the universe is probably teaming with intelligent life. As a result you may become more socially progressive and value better education, health care, expanded human rights, and fairness more than ever because you value humanity more than ever.

- Ironically, you may be a little less sociable because you want time to ponder life more. You may take up meditation and value your quiet time each day. You may be more introspective and health conscious. Your daily interactions may change, and you may avoid angry or ignorant people. People don't seem to upset you as easily as before. You become kinder, more tolerant, more patient, and more joyous. Life seems easier!

- You may prefer to spend time and money on developing yourself more rather than acquiring many material things. You may attend conferences and seminars.

- You may realize that the Earth, with its millions of different species, may be a jewel in the cosmos, and you begin to feel strongly about preserving the environment. As you learn about environmental impacts and how the universe works, you realize that *we are all spiritually and energetically connected.* You consider this a fact, rather than New Age mumbo jumbo, and alter your beliefs and lifestyle accordingly.

- With a belief in NHI now firmly rooted in your psyche, you may question the accuracy of the religion you were taught: that version of God may feel small to you. You may relinquish a belief in a personal God who doles out punishment or rewards. You may relinquish beliefs in heaven or hell as actual places but still believe that consciousness continues after death. You may start to read ancient texts regarding reincarnation, the origins of religions, and how the earliest NHI may have influenced religion. You may start to believe in an impersonal God that pervades all things, pervades each atom in the universe, and with whom we can cocreate the power of our intent, emotions, and mind. Things you may have considered sacred in the past may no longer feel sacred to you, and things you never imagined as sacred will feel more sacred to you. You may consider God to be much larger and pervasive than ever before.

- You may consider the existence of multiple dimensions or universes. You may be awed by the idea of an intelligent universe that is constantly expanding, and you may realize that as our thoughts expand, the universe likewise expands, and we each have an important role in that expansion! You may suspect that the atoms of the universe are intelligent and that consciousness pervades all things.
- You may start respecting your body more and taking better care of it.
- You may develop greatly expanded intuition, such as clairvoyance or healing abilities. Refer to Chapter 9 for more information on these topics.

You may recalibrate your identity, belief system, and worldview, which results in peace, awe, appreciation, and acceptance of NHI entities. This recalibration may take years to solidify and will result in psychological and spiritual maturation, a sense of wonder about the cosmos, a sense of unity with others, and a sense of strength and joy as you better understand the expanding universe. Ultimately, you may be grateful for *that moment* that changed your life.

CHAPTER 4 QUESTIONNAIRE:
WHAT STAGE ARE YOU IN?

Use this questionnaire to help you determine the primary stage you are in at a given time. Answer true or false for each question based on how you mostly feel at this moment in time. For example, you may think you feel both true and false to a statement depending on the day, but respond to how you feel right now. There are no right or wrong answers. Remember, you will flip between stages and visit each stage multiple times, so this questionnaire is meant to be a guidepost that changes over time. You may want to take it multiple times during your journey. Refer to the scoring at the end of the questionnaire.

1. When I think about NHI entities, I am awestruck by its vast implications. *(5 points)*
2. I avoid thinking about my experience because it is just too far-fetched. *(1 point)*
3. It seems hard to believe that the entire world does not acknowledge NHI entities. *(3 points)*
4. So much of what I used to believe just doesn't make sense now. *(5 points)*
5. Now I think I understand how we are all connected. *(5 points)*
6. I jump at every little shadow now! *(1 point)*
7. The more I release old beliefs, the more wondrous the universe seems. *(5 points)*
8. I have to pretend my experience never happened, or I'll go crazy. *(1 point)*
9. I didn't know learning about UFOs and NHI entities would be a new hobby! *(3 points)*
10. When I think of UFOs and NHI entities, I am very intrigued. *(3 points)*
11. I must have just imagined my experience. *(1 point)*

CONTINUES

12. It is okay if I don't know all the answers now. I'll feel better when I learn more. *(5 points)*

13. When I think about my experience, I am enraged! *(2 points)*

14. I had a weird dream, and now I'm going overboard with a bunch of kooky ideas. *(1 point)*

15. My old religion doesn't seem to make sense now. *(5 points)*

16. I can't sleep at night because I am so afraid of NHI entities coming again. *(2 points)*

17. It is not fair that this experience happened to me! I deserve better! *(2 points)*

18. I want to forget about this whole topic and go back to my old life. *(1 point)*

19. Why did NHI entities take me? *(3 points)*

20. Why aren't these topics all over the news? *(3 points)*

21. Since my experience, I'm so paranoid. *(2 points)*

22. How dare NHI entities take me and violate my human rights! *(2 points)*

23. This can't be real. Aliens don't exist, or we would have been told about them. *(1 point)*

24. My thoughts directly influence my reality. *(5 points)*

25. I don't know what to believe anymore. *(5 points)*

26. I'm terrified NHI entities will come back again. *(2 points)*

27. It feels as if I have one foot in two different worlds—my old world and this new world. *(5 points)*

28. I'm going to forget about the whole experience and just get on with my old life. *(1 point)*

29. The enormity of the universe is staggering, and it is all connected. *(5 points)*

30. I can't live with this experience. Every day and night is hell. *(2 points)*

31. Nothing I believed in before seems right now. I don't know what to think. *(5 points)*

32. If NHI entities are real, what about other entities, like fairies, Bigfoot, or ghosts? *(3 points)*

33. Are NHI entities going to kidnap me again and keep me this time? *(2 points)*

34. I feel so alone and disconnected from my friends and family. *(3 points)*

35. Something very weird happened to me, and I can't live with it. *(1 point)*

36. I had a nightmare, and now I'm getting hysterical about it. I need to get a grip! *(1 point)*

37. I wish I had more time to learn about UFOs and NHI entities. *(3 points)*

38. I can't sleep or concentrate on anything, and now I'm messing up at work. *(1 point)*

39. I know I encountered NHI entities, but I can never tell anyone. *(3 points)*

40. I want to be alone to sort this out and learn more about NHI entities, but life gets in the way. *(3 points)*

41. Sometimes I feel very connected to the Earth. *(5 points)*

42. UFOs and NHI entities are the most amazing things in the history of the world! *(3 points)*

43. I just want to go away and sleep. *(1 point)*

44. How can this have happened to me? Nothing will ever be the same again! *(1 point)*

45. I must be going crazy to have imagined such an experience. *(1 point)*

Scoring Chart

15–30 points: You are mainly in the Shock and Denial stage.

30–45 points: You are mainly in the Fear and Anger stage.

45–60 points: You are mainly in the Exploration and Isolation stage.

Over 60 points: You are mainly in the Relinquishment and Recalibration stage.

Chapter 5

WHAT SOCIAL RESEARCHERS HAVE LEARNED ABOUT CONTACT

Kathleen Marden

Imagine this: you are viewing a television show on UFOs, when a well-meaning skeptic offers a prosaic explanation for your abduction memories. He informs viewers that the complex imagery that has been haunting you for years has a simple explanation. It is all related to sleep paralysis and sleep-related hallucinations that occur when factors such as stress, extreme fatigue, and medications cause the part of your brain that distinguishes between conscious perceptions and internally generated perceptions to misfire. You've already heard other so-called experts argue that your nocturnal experiences are based in birth trauma, narcolepsy, the last movie you watched, the things you learned from a supportive therapist, or the hypnosis sessions you had. Perhaps you are fantasy prone. Maybe your personality disorder is at the root of your problems. Or perhaps you have "false memory syndrome." A sleep specialist sends you to a sleep lab but can find no abnormality in your sleep patterns—no evidence of narcolepsy, no frontal lobe disorders. If only you could take a pill and all of this would end . . . would you?

Several high-profile UFO abduction cases during the 1970s initiated a search for the psychosocial roots of alien abduction. The momentum increased in the 1980s and 1990s when reports emerged from individuals claiming to have been kidnapped by nonhumans while they slept in their own beds. The amorphous nature of bedroom abductions led well-meaning academic psychologists to search for answers through a succession of studies on self-identified alien abductees. Additionally, skeptical psychologists dished up purported psychological features that could lead to the so-called misguided belief that UFOs and alien abductions are real. They offered the general public hypothetical explanations such as mental illness, personality disorders, fantasy proneness, "false memory syndrome," confabulation under hypnosis, sleep anomalies, and absorption of the prevailing cultural mythos. Investigative reports that documented missing time following a conscious close encounter with an unconventional craft, conscious recall of nonhuman entities—sometimes by more than one witness, the PTSD that is sometimes related to an abduction experience, anomalous marks on experiencers' bodies, correlating data from multiple witnesses who have undergone hypnosis to lift amnesia, and so on, were usually ignored by biased researchers. However, not all research was biased. This chapter focuses on some of these studies and the information researchers have learned through a series of surveys.

Years of systematic study by academic psychologists have left us with one conclusion: self-identified alien abductees exhibit no more psychopathology than the general population. In the absence of a primary psychiatric disorder, experimental psychologists have searched for alternative psychological explanations. Several experimental studies over the past thirty years have attempted to delineate personality traits that separate UFO abduction experiencers from nonexperiencers, such as boundary deficit disorder, borderline personality disorder, schizotypal personality disorder, fantasy proneness, and dissociative identity disorder.

People with personality disorders carry certain socially distressing traits throughout their lifetime, which may fluctuate in terms of symptoms and intensity. The carriers of these traits exhibit negative, hostile, needy, or antisocial behavior. Their needy, attention-seeking behavior propels them toward a host of mental health professionals, UFO researchers, and paranormal investigators who eventually, for their own well-being, step off the roller-coaster ride. These emotional vampires have an uncanny ability to zap your energy.

The first formal psychological study to evaluate the mental health of abductees was carried out in 1985 by Elizabeth Slater, a clinical psychologist. The five male and four female participants in the study had been recommended to Slater by UFO researchers Budd Hopkins and Ted Bloecher and psychotherapist Aphrodite Clamar. Slater did not know that the persons she administered a battery of psychological tests to felt they had been abducted by aliens. Slater discovered that the group exhibited high intellect and "highly evocative inner worlds."[1] They were emotionally immature, egocentric, highly creative, inventive types with lower self-esteem and identity disturbance. However, their abduction experiences could not be attributed to mental disorders. They had none of the characteristics of multiple personality disorder or schizophrenia, nor were they pathological liars.

THE OMEGA PROJECTS

The Omega Project was a psychological survey of persons reporting abductions and other UFO encounters conducted by Kenneth Ring and Christopher J. Rosing from the University of Connecticut in 1990. This large study of 264 participants included four distinct groups: (1) an abductee group, (2) a near-death experiencers (NDE) group, (3) a control group of individuals who only expressed an interest in UFOs, and (4) a control group with an interest in NDEs. The participants completed a battery of personality screenings designed to assess the psychological factors that give some individuals the propensity to experience UFO abductions and to compare them to near-death experiencers.

The study discovered that UFO and near-death experiencers are similar because both groups developed increased psychic awareness, altruistic feelings, and increased spirituality as a result of their experiences. They found that both experiencer groups were no more fantasy prone than the control groups. Additionally, the abductee and NDE groups reported having childhood sensitivity to psychic phenomena, nonphysical beings, and alternate realities (the ability to see into other realities or to see beings that others are not aware of).

Both experiencer groups reported a significantly higher level of childhood abuse and trauma. There was an increased level of serious illness during childhood as well. The researchers discovered an increased level of dissociation as a coping mechanism among both experiencer groups, but it was higher in the UFO abductee group. The researchers suggested that childhood abuse could have set up the conditions for children to develop the psychological defense of splitting off from the source of the threat and tuning into other realities. These other realities offer a safety net that separates the abused children from the harm that is being inflicted upon them.

The Omega Project researchers concluded their study with the following statement:

> Our sample as a whole appears to regard UFOs and NDEs positively and we believe that they hold out potential benefits for humanity that we can hardly conceive of today. . . .

However, the data from the Omega Project, and especially those on beliefs and values, strongly suggest that these experiences also contain a powerful impetus for a variety of healthy and positive changes. Psychiatric categories shouldn't obscure the transformative potential of these experiencers and, in our opinion, the positive evaluation that respondents tend to place on their experiences may show that their sometimes-traumatic impact is less important than their long-term transformative promise.[2]

The Omega Study's UFO experiencer and NDE groups reported a significantly increased level of malfunctions in electrical equipment following an experience. This has long been known as a marker of alien abduction/contact. It was significantly elevated in the Marden-Stoner Commonalities Study and the most recent MUFON Experiencer Study. Experiencers in both groups reported malfunctions in electrical appliances. Lights blink out when experiencers walk under them; watches, computers, store scanners, and time clocks malfunction only for the experiencers.

Dr. Robert LeLieuvre, Lester Valez, and Michael Freeman spearheaded their own Omega Project called "Omega 3" in 2010. Valez was MUFON's Director of Abduction Research at the time, and the study was done under the auspices of MUFON. Its objective was to test Ring and Rosen's Omega Project findings. Seventy-one abduction experiencers and fifty-one people with an interest in abduction phenomena, but no direct contact, comprised the experiential and control groups. Eight of the psychological instruments used in the first Omega Project study and two by Canadian academic researcher Michael Persinger were used in the study to test physiological, psychological, and philosophical areas.

MUFON's Omega Project found that the participants in both groups were no more fantasy prone than the general population.

However, the experiential group demonstrated a greater interest in alien contact, and this interest changed the participants' worldview. They became more sensitive to altered states of consciousness and reported early psi experiences; psychosocial tension as children; higher rates of stress, conflict, and tension as adults; greater tendencies toward dissociation as a coping mechanism; a shift toward spiritual beliefs; and concerns for our planet's ecology. The researchers stated that their study does *not* suggest that ET contact is imaginary.

In the mid-1980s, PhD candidate June Parnell and her supervising professor Leo Sprinkle conducted a study on 225 individuals at the University of Wyoming to identify the personality characteristics of those who reported UFO experiences. They used the Minnesota Multiphasic Personality Inventory (MMPI), a screening designed to assess psychopathology, and the Sixteen Personality Factors Questionaire (16PF), an assessment of healthy personality functioning. The participants included four groups: (1) individuals who made no claim of observing a UFO, (2) a group who reported observing spacecraft or UFO occupants, (3) a group who claimed to have been taken aboard a spacecraft, and (4) a group who claimed to have communicated with UFO occupants.

The psychologists were primarily interested in the psychological profiles of experiencers on four scales: (1) scale F on the MMPI that measures unusual attitudes, feelings, or thoughts; (2) scale 8 on the MMPI that measures divergent thinking, creativity or schizoid tendencies, and alienation; (3) scale 9 on the MMPI that measures unstable mood, flight of ideas, and psychomotor activity; and (4) factor M on the 16PF scale that could indicate tendencies toward fantasy proneness, imaginative thoughts, absentmindedness, or bohemian behavior.

The study discovered that participants who reported UFO and/or occupant sightings scored within the normal range of functioning on scale 8. They were described as reserved, intelligent, assertive, experimenting, liberal, free-thinking, self-sufficient, resourceful, and independent. However, those who reported communication with ETs had moderately elevated scores for unusual feelings and thoughts. They were characterized as having elevated levels of interpersonal sensitivity, moral self-righteousness, suspiciousness, and creative or schizoid tendencies. They also cared greatly about what others thought of them.

Both groups scored within the normal range of functioning on scale 9, indicating that they did not exhibit psychopathology regarding mood stability, rational thought, and psychomotor activity—behavioral characteristics that are common in mental illness. Likewise, factor M on the 16PF scale revealed that even those who reported occupant sightings and communication with ETs performed within the normal range on items such as fantasy proneness, imaginative thoughts, absentmindedness, and bohemian behavior. The psychologists suggested that the two categories of elevated scores might be viewed as an endorsement of this more bizarre experience and not an indication of psychopathology.

THE 1991 ROPER POLL

In 1991 UFO and abduction researchers Budd Hopkins, a distinguished abstract expressionist artist and UFO abduction researcher from New York City, and David Jacobs, associate professor of history at Temple University, developed a series of eleven questions that were designed to obtain statistical data on the percentage of Americans that had been abducted by aliens. Through funding by Robert Bigelow from the Bigelow Aerospace Corporation, their questions were added to a Roper poll. Later in the study, Ron Westrum, a professor of sociology and specialist in the sociology of science and technology at Eastern Michigan University, participated.

A representative sample of 5,947 Americans participated in the poll with regard to unusual personal experiences. They included seeing a ghost, seeing a UFO, seeing a terrifying figure (such as a witch, monster, or devil), and having an out-of-body experience. The nonsense word *Trondant* was introduced to identify hoaxers and delusional participants, and they were excluded from the final analysis. The following five markers for alien abduction were presented:

1. Waking up paralyzed with the sense of a strange person, presence, or something else in the room
2. Feeling that you were actually flying through the air, although you didn't know why or how
3. Experiencing a period of time of an hour or more, in which you were apparently lost, but you could not remember why or where you had been
4. Seeing unusual lights or balls of light in a room without knowing what was causing them, or where they came from
5. Finding puzzling scars on your body and neither you nor anyone else could remember how you received them or where you got them[3]

Participants were directed to indicate if their experiences had happened more than twice, once or twice, or never. Over seventeen years, they interviewed nearly 500 experiencers with these commonalities, so Hopkins and Jacobs felt confident that anyone who answered four of the five questions with a positive response had the markers for a UFO abduction. At the end of the survey, 2 percent, or 119 survey participants, had all four key markers for alien abduction, and some reported all five of them. Based on the survey results, Hopkins predicted that 3.7 million Americans met the criteria for a real alien abduction.

Researchers, such as myself, who have spent years interviewing experiencers, know that the five markers for alien abduction are closely tied to abduction/contact phenomena and have been reported time and time again by experiencers. However, there were errors in the construction of two of their questions. They were not specific enough, and they failed to ask only one question per sentence. This led to ridicule and derision by skeptical scientists and writers, some of whom refused to read the research report. Others cited methodological flaws and the errors.

Question 1 was flawed because waking up paralyzed with the sense of a presence in the room is an indicator of sleep paralysis. Having shadowy figures looming overhead and a feeling of terror is a common characteristic of sleep paralysis as well. However, we can be certain that sleep paralysis is not present when an experiencer is awake and can move his or her body and observes an entity in the room.

PERSONALITY STUDIES

In 1993, Nicholas Spanos, Patricia Cross, Kirby Dickson, and Susan DuBreuil of Carleton University administered an extensive battery of scales to nineteen individuals who reported observing erratically moving lights in the sky that they interpreted as UFOs and twenty individuals who reported experiencing a close encounter and/or abduction by nonhuman entities. They discovered that UFO reporters, missing time experiencers, and those who believe they have communicated telepathically with aliens are no more fantasy prone than the general population. However, those with higher scores on the fantasy proneness scale reported more elaborate abduction experiences.

In a larger personality study in 1993, they administered five psychometric scales to 176 test subjects, who were divided into four groups. Group 1 had observed a UFO close up and/or experienced a period of missing time; Group 2 had seen unusual lights in the sky; Group 3 was a control group that had no UFO-related experiences; and Group 4 was composed of graduate students who denied having seen a UFO. Twenty psychological tests were administered to the four groups. Test results revealed that the experiential groups exhibited lower schizophrenia, higher self-esteem, higher well-being, lower perceptual aberration, lower perception of an unfriendly world, lower aggression, and no difference from the control groups in social strength. Additional testing revealed no difference between the control and experiential groups in absorption, fantasy proneness, and the tendency to engage in imaginings. Spanos concluded that the experiential groups were not psychologically disturbed. The only factor that distinguished them from the control groups was their belief that they had observed UFOs and alien life forms.

Numerous academic psychological studies have been carried out over the past forty years. I could detail all of them in this book, but in the interest of presenting new studies by UFO researchers, I will not labor upon them. You can read my research paper on the older studies under the heading "Essays on ET Contact" at *www.kathleen -marden.com*.

THE MUFON EXPERIENCER SURVEY

MUFON's Experiencer Research Team completed a comprehensive multiyear study (2015–2018) on UFO abduction and contact experiencers. ERT members Craig Lang, MS (1956–2018); Michael Austin Melton, PhD; Denise Stoner; and I developed 118 questions for the Experiencer Survey. We used SurveyMonkey, an online application that is readily available to participants and automatically calculates statistical data.

The greatest problem with a survey of this type is the inability to measure the psychological functioning of its participants and the veracity of the statistical data, given the opportunity for hoaxers and delusional people to participate in the study. We developed several trick questions to identify this category of participant. The questions were carefully worded and presented to prevent false positive or false negative responses.

Our objective was to pinpoint a host of characteristics that experiencers have in common and to collect statistical data that would be of value to MUFON investigators, researchers, and experiencers alike. Our target group was UFO abduction and contact experiencers who retained conscious recall of the nonhuman entities they encountered and the procedures performed in an alien environment. This was clearly stated in the informed consent agreement. It also advised participants that they might experience increased anxiety due to the nature of the questions. The Experiencer Survey link was posted on MUFON's website and on my website in late July 2015.

The study was advertised in the *MUFON UFO Journal,* on my Facebook page, and on some of my radio interviews. MUFON's ERT encouraged the experiencers they counseled to complete the survey if they met the criteria for participation. We intentionally did not elicit participation from contactees who practiced astral travel, conscious contact with nonphysical entities, remote viewing, and drug-induced contact.

Our questions were straightforward and pertained to the abduction/contact experience, based on our investigative findings, the historical findings of other investigators, the psychological research findings in a variety of academic studies, and the postulates offered by prominent skeptics. The minimum target for statistical analysis was set at 500 participants. (See the full report of the MUFON 2018 International Symposium Proceedings and Kathleen's presentation, available at *https://mufon.z2systems.com/np/clients/mufon/giftstore .jsp.*)

Phase 2 of our study was completed by Dr. Don C. Donderi, a retired psychologist and statistician from McGill University. He administered the American Personality Inventory (API) to 188 survey participants that agreed to take part in the next phase of our survey. The API was developed by Ted Davis, a clinical social worker, and abduction researcher Budd Hopkins as an indicator of UFO Abduction Syndrome. Davis and Hopkins used the well-known psychological measure MMPI (mentioned earlier in this chapter) as a model for the API. Dr. Donderi collaborated with them by enlisting the help of students at McGill for the control groups and on its evaluation.

They obtained responses to 608 true/false questions from fifty-two self-reported abductees and compared their responses to seventy-five nonabductee controls and twenty-six simulators who knew the characteristics pertaining to UFO abductions but had not had an experience themselves. A subset of sixty-five questions was identified for the standardized measure after Dr. Donderi completed his statistical analysis of the three groups' responses.

We were surprised to find that Dr. Donderi's API analysis in phase 2 of MUFON's study did not yield the anticipated results. No one obtained a score close to the simulator or nonabductee targets. Many scored close to the abductee target, but others were distributed along a wide range in reference to the target. I offered the speculation that perhaps modern experiencers have engaged in positive contact and do not exhibit the symptoms of UFO Abduction Syndrome. For this reason, Dr. Donderi and I decided to compare the responses of the twenty highest scorers to the twenty lowest scorers in an effort to identify differences between the two groups. The twenty participants who scored closest to the target were identified as the "abductee group" because they met the criteria for UFO Abduction Syndrome. The twenty lowest scorers were labeled the "contactee group" because the majority indicated that their contact was positive. However, five members of this group reported contact of a highly negative nature.

The Experiencer Survey participants were evenly divided between men and women, as was the abductee group. However, the contactee group had fourteen males and six females. We received completed surveys from participants residing in seven different time zones around the globe. Ten ethnic groups and many mixed-race groups were represented. Age groups ranged from under twenty to over eighty, but the highest percentage of the distribution was in the forty to fifty-nine range.

We posed the question, "What age were you when you had your first experience?" The survey takers indicated that 72 percent were less than twenty when first contacted. The number was 80 percent for the abductee group and 70 percent for the contactees. This response rate is consistent with the current view of generational contact and confirms the anecdotal evidence offered by many.

Surprisingly, 6 percent of the survey takers and 15 percent of the contactees stated that they were more than forty years old when their first experience took place. In our final analysis, we discovered that the small group of experiencers who were over forty at the time of their first experience have a special set of characteristics that are not present in the abductees whose contacts began early in life. Their experiences were primarily negative and frequent. These wretched souls are repeatedly taken to a dreadful environment where they are physically and sexually abused or forced to train for what they believe is intergalactic war. They do not share the commonalities that other experiencers share. I do not have additional information that can assess the psychological profile of this perplexing group of primarily male individuals. I know only that they do not have UFO Abduction Syndrome and do not have the commonalities that other experiencers share.

We were surprised to discover that more than half (54 percent) of the survey takers believed they had been taken fewer than four times and 24 percent believe it was only once. A full 10 percent believed they had been taken more than fifty times. This response was a surprise, as the common wisdom indicated that the majority of experiencers had been taken many times.

Those with UFO Abduction Syndrome reported an elevated number of abduction experiences. Their responses are as follows: five to nine times: 20 percent; ten to nineteen times: 15 percent; twenty+ times: 10 percent; fifty+ times: 5 percent. This increased rate is indicative of what one might expect if a group of scientists were carrying out a research project.

Those who scored furthest away from the UFO Abduction Syndrome target had unique responses: 45 percent indicated that they had been contacted only once, and a surprising 15 percent believed they had been contacted more than fifty times. As we move along, you will become aware of the unique characteristics that the older first contact and multiple contact experiencers share.

With regard to the observation of UFOs, 85 percent of the survey takers indicated that they had conscious recall of a UFO sighting. In comparison, 90 percent of the abductee group and 95 percent of the contactee group stated they had observed a UFO. We know that a UFO is an unidentified flying object and can be only a perplexing but distant light in the sky. For this reason, we wanted to know if the UFO was 500 feet or less from the witness, indicating a close encounter. To this question, 65 percent of the survey takers said they had conscious recall of observing a UFO within 500 feet of their physical location. Among the abductee group, the number was 70 percent. This number increased to 85 percent for the contactee group. The fact that the three groups observed structured craft at close range is important. Many people report distant lights in the sky, but close encounters are not as prevalent.

Sighting an NHI entity and retaining conscious recall of the sighting is far less prevalent. However, 54 percent of the survey takers, 50 percent of the abductee group, and 55 percent of the contactee group stated that they had observed an NHI entity. One of our prerequisites for participation in the survey was conscious recall of observing NHI entities, so we were surprised when only half of our participants followed the written instructions.

We were interested in the prevalence of generational contact among experiencers, as common wisdom tells us that it follows family lines. In regard to this issue, 50 percent of the survey takers indicated that their family members had a close encounter, and 41 percent had relatives who had experienced abduction/contact. Generational contact is more prevalent in the abductee group, with 60 percent reporting generational close encounters and contact with NHI entities. The contactee group said that 60 percent had family members who had a close encounter. However, the rate was only 30 percent for generational contact with NHI entities.

The most frequently cited family members for close encounters and contact, in all three groups, were the mothers and fathers, followed by their brothers and sisters. Their offspring and their grandparents were also mentioned, but in lower numbers. Could this lower percentage mean that the NHI entities are closing out their experimental program? Or could the experiencers be unaware that their children have been taken? Only time will tell.

We posed two questions pertaining to sleep paralysis. The first question identified the characteristics of sleep paralysis that occur in a percentage of the general population and may not be related to abduction/contact. In this case, 74 percent of survey takers, 90 percent for the abductee group, and 65 percent for the contactee group answered in the affirmative.

When asked if they had been awake but then saw a nonhuman entity and became unable to move or cry out, 36 percent of the survey takers said yes. The percentage of wakeful contact increased dramatically to 60 percent in the abductee group and dropped to 25 percent in the contactee group. The highly significant statistic for the abductee group could be an indication that their events are real. This an important marker for nocturnal contact in the home.

Many experiencers report that they can sense when contact is imminent. In this case, 48 percent of the survey takers, 60 percent for the abductee group, and 35 percent for the contactee group had this feeling. Of the abductee group, 90 percent reported that they hear buzzing, chirping, or tinnitus sounds in their heads as a precursor to contact; 64 percent feel nervous, and 50 percent feel what they describe as "energy."

MUFON's statistics on missing time indicated that 58 percent of the survey takers were aware of at least one period of lost time that they believed was ET contact related. Missing time was noted by 65 percent of the abductee group. However, only 45 percent of the contactee group was aware of missing time associated with ET contact. The duration of the missing time experience was slightly elevated at two hours among abductees, which is consistent with the findings of other researchers.

There has been much discussion about the demeanor of NHI entities. Strong emotions have come into play at both ends of the spectrum with much promotion of the evil alien and benevolent alien perspectives. Our study determined that the most prevalent response was "business-like" for survey takers (48 percent) and the abductee group (65 percent). The contactee group had a different opinion. Their contact experiences were "kind" and "friendly" (50 percent). The abductees stated that demeanor varied by type with some races being more caring than others. Less than 11 percent in all three groups stated they had encountered evil entities and less than 6 percent said they were hostile or sadistic. An appraisal of the statements made by highly negative contact experiencers led

Betty's Grey *(courtesy of Kathleen Marden)*

me to speculate that some individuals might be under the control of highly negative entities from the astral realm. (The astral realm is a theoretical plane of nonphysical existence inhabited by the ethereal bodies of humans between physical lives on Earth.) One participant's responses indicated that he was probably taken by shapeshifting Reptilians. Two had memories of being trained regularly for intragalactic war. Another clearly believed he was having MILAB (military) abductions by humans dressed in Air Force uniforms, Reptilians, and eight other entity types. He indicated that he had been harassed by Men in Black and threatened by a government agent. He also had a high level of paranormal activity in his home.

Our study could not determine if these memories have a psychological overlay. Perhaps some individuals have been kidnapped by highly negative, even evil entities who feast on human fear and loathing. This small group of negative contact experiencers mentioned mind control and being forced to harm others. But additional investigation and psychological screenings will have to determine the validity of these claims. MUFON's Experiencer Survey did not measure psychological functioning.

The bulk of the contactee group reported an elevated level of kind, friendly contact. Most felt honored and pleased by the highly spiritual, benevolent nature of their events. Likewise, a small but significant percentage of the abductee group had engaged in contact of a positive nature.

Let's compare the entity types that interacted with each of the three experiencer groups. We first asked for descriptive details such as height, color, clothing or no clothing, clothing color, and the like. We then listed seventeen known categories of entities, leaving room for "unknown" and "other" responses. Many experiencers have reported interactions with more than one entity type, so we allowed for as many responses as the participants needed. We discovered that Greys were the most frequently reported NHI entity type. Greys in the 4'5"–5'5" height range were most frequently reported. Greys above 5'5" were next among the three groups of experiencers. Average human types were a close third for all but the contactee group. They mentioned Tall Whites at a higher rate, which probably accounts for the friendly demeanor of their NHI entities' contact. Less than 25 percent of all three groups mentioned Mantis Insectoid types; less than 20 percent for lizard type Reptilians; and less than 13 percent for draconian type Reptilians. The abductee group mentioned hybrids (27 percent) at a higher rate than the other two groups, which fell below 20 percent. Human types of tall and short varieties came in at less than 10 percent, as did Tall

Goldens, Tall Blues, Short Blues, and Sasquatch types. In addition to the nonhuman entity types, several groups were listed in small numbers. They include light beings, blue humanoid avians, cat-like, and black-cloaked beings.

MILAB abductions were tested under a separate category. The survey takers indicated that 13 percent had participated in MILAB abductions. This number declined to 10 percent for the abductee and contactee groups. All groups failed to clearly identify the uniform of the human military groups and the race(s) of the nonhuman entities they observed. This is somewhat troubling, primarily because conspiracy theorists have promoted the idea that "black ops" military groups are abducting humans from their homes and using mind control on them. Our findings might suggest that NHI entities are masquerading as human military officers, thus impugning our armed forces and feeding into conspiracy theory.

One form of evidence that is most frequently submitted by experiencers to investigators is strange marks on their bodies for which they can think of no commonplace explanation. The most commonly reported marks are finger-shaped bruises, puncture wounds, and cored-out circular marks, referred to as "scoop marks." Also mentioned were burned or cored-out triangles, blistering burns, and etchings.

When the three groups were asked if they would end their abduction/contact events if they could, 71 percent of the survey takers (N:479) said they would *not* want to end their contact events. The statistic was 75 percent for both the abductee and contactee groups. However, a significant percentage of participants in all three groups could not make a firm decision. They offered equivocal remarks, such as it is not their decision, they agreed to this before they were born, and they would continue if it is for the benefit of humanity and the NHI entities.

We asked a variety of questions pertaining to the health issues that have been documented in abduction cases. Overall, 53 percent of the survey takers indicated that they had experienced health problems they believed were related to their abduction/contact events. Immediately following an abduction/contact experience, sinus problems and migraine headaches were the most commonly mentioned health issues faced by survey takers. Nosebleeds and eye irritation were also common. As reported in the Marden-Stoner study, there is an elevated level of chronic fatigue and immune dysfunction syndrome among experiencers. The statistic was 38 percent in the Marden-Stoner study and remained high in MUFON's experiencer study.

Many abductees have reported being healed by NHI entities, and some have submitted medical confirmation of their diagnosis and spontaneous remission following an alleged visitation. As mentioned in Chapter 3, Jim's lymph nodes became tiny and necrotic following an orb event in his bedroom. In 2012, I was healed from medically diagnosed Chronic Fatigue Immune Dysfunction Syndrome (CFIDS) when an experiencer requested healing for me. I have submitted my evidence to a medical doctor who is conducting research on miraculous healings. We wondered how prevalent alleged healings by NHI entities are among the experiencer population. Only 10 percent of the survey takers said they had been healed by NHI entities. The statistic was significantly elevated at 45 percent for the abductee group but declined to 10 percent for the contactee group. Perhaps the reason is that NHI entities have a special interest in caring for the humans they have abducted.

With regard to the prevalence of paranormal activity in the homes of experiencers, 61 percent of the survey takers reported seeing lighted orbs in their homes. This number declined to 50 percent for the abductee group and 45 percent for the contactee group.

We asked, "Did you participate in a religious faith prior to your abduction/contact event?" This question tested a hypothesis that has been advanced by some religious leaders: the absence of a Godly covering among experiencers has left them vulnerable to contact by the minions of Satan. We discovered that 45 percent of the survey takers, 55 percent of the abductees, and 70 percent of the contactees participated in a religious faith prior to contact.

Experiencers in general indicated that they became more spiritual as a result of contact. The statistics for the three groups are as follows: survey takers, 69 percent; abductee group, 86 percent; contactee group, 71 percent. This response indicates that although many adhered to existing religious doctrine, they also trended toward spiritual development, an interest in life beyond the physical, and the sacred meaning of life. It does not indicate the absence of God in their lives. For most, it signifies a deeper personal relationship with God, the One, or the Creator, and a slight trend away from traditional religious doctrine.

I believe it is important to note that MUFON discovered an increased level of near-death experiences on the Experiencer Survey. Among MUFON's three groups, 44 percent of the survey takers stated they'd had a near-death experience. In the abductee group, the level increased to 55 percent, whereas in the contactee group, the level decreased to 35 percent. These findings are consistent with the Omega Project studies that noted psychic awareness, altruistic feelings, and increased spirituality among NDE and UFO experiencers.

My personal search for understanding has led me to theoretical physics. If it is true that experiencers undergo the process of dematerializing or phasing into another reality during the transition from our physical environment to an alien environment, it stands to reason that their soul consciousness might fragment off from their physical structure or be attached only by a thread. This fracturing is similar to what near-death experiencers endure, even though the causation might be different. If my supposition is correct, it could explain the reason why UFO and NDE groups exhibit similar characteristics.

We asked open-ended questions pertaining to warnings about future apocalyptic or disastrous events and other information that the nonhumans had imparted to survey takers. The majority of survey takers had not received specific information. However, 159 had. The following is a representative sample of replies from all three groups regarding humanity's future:

- "We must unite together in love and raise our vibration as a collective. The higher dimensions are here assisting us. We must unite together and recognize we are all connected so we can evolve and access Christ-consciousness through the fifth dimension."
- "If we raise our level of consciousness to a higher level, we are able to achieve more. This is what they are trying to do here. We have been to this position before and we destroyed ourselves. They are fearful that we are in a position to do that again, and they will not allow it this time. They will intervene."
- "They are here to guide and assist in the development of our species and our world. They planted our seed here and they helped to develop it. They introduce things to assist in our development."
- "Humans must regain their spiritual sovereignty. Humans are created by God, like them. Not sinful."
- "We need to take responsibility for our actions and love one another."
- "They are spiritually connected and the human experience is a spiritual progression."

- "They are here to assist humanity in raising its vibrational frequency."

There were also many cautionary remarks issued with regard to our stewardship of planet Earth. Here are a few:

- "I was told that we have to preserve resources and if we don't, we will experience a decrease in population."
- "We are poisoning our world and all that live on it. If we don't change the way we live as a species, we all die."
- "We are destroying our planet. They will interfere with force if we continue our aggression and war."
- "Ice caps melting and endangered species dying off. It was incredibly difficult to watch."
- "I was told that ecological catastrophic events were on the horizon due to exponential effects of our neglect, abuse, or misuse."
- "I saw a barren Earth. And I was told repeatedly about protecting nature and the importance of human unity."
- "We, as a race, are burning through resources faster than we can renew them. Due to our arrogance, we will seek out resources elsewhere, but because we are arrogant and ego driven, we'll try to acquire them at a heavy cost to other races."
- "Humans will become extinct if they do not change their destructive and polluting ways."
- "We are not at the end of times; we are at the beginning of a New Age. So much cleansing needs to take place on the earth herself and in people. It's time to unite."

Regardless of the causative factors behind their experiences and the attitudinal changes they generate, a significant number of survey takers in all three groups indicated that they have benefited from their experiences. Only a small percentage of participants indicated that they have experienced highly negative contact. Overall, they have become more spiritual, more empathic, more psychic or intuitive, and less oriented toward aggression, negativity, and the acquisition of material goods. They care for the environment and are concerned about making planet Earth a better place for all.

CHAPTER 5 CHECKLIST: ARE YOU AN ABDUCTEE, A CONTACTEE, OR NEITHER?

Use the following checklist to help you determine if you are a classic abductee or contactee. Check each box that applies to you. Tally the boxes in each category that you have checked. You are an abductee if you checked off more boxes in the abductee category than in the contactee category. You are a contactee if you checked off more boxes in the contactee category than in the abductee category.

Are you an abductee? *(Check all that apply.)*

☐ Younger than nineteen years old when first taken
☐ Four to nine experiences
☐ Rh– blood type but might be Rh+
☐ Other family members have been abducted
☐ Religious and spiritual
☐ Had a close encounter when outside
☐ Have conscious recall of seeing a craft
☐ Awake when taken from home
☐ Remember being in a craft
☐ Recurring dreams of abduction
☐ Sense when you are going to be taken
☐ Hear buzzing sounds in your head and feel nervous before being taken
☐ Receive telepathic messages and downloads of information
☐ Feel electrical tingling
☐ Find puncture wounds and incisions
☐ Have a suspected implant
☐ Have difficulty sleeping, but don't attribute it to fear of abduction
☐ Are happy and stable
☐ Have felt motion in your mattress as if something unseen is walking on it

CONTINUES

- ☐ Have seen lighted orbs floating in your home
- ☐ Are intuitive or psychic
- ☐ Have been healed by ETs or can heal others
- ☐ Have been informed about environmental changes and the possibility of global war
- ☐ Have had a near-death experience
- ☐ Believe the ETs are mostly business-like
- ☐ Have been taken by Greys or Insectoids
- ☐ Have a high degree of empathy for others
- ☐ Feel a sense of universal connectedness
- ☐ Have higher than average environmental awareness
- ☐ Are an empath
- ☐ Have thought about seeking support

Are you a contactee? *(Check all that apply.)*

- ☐ No other family members have been abducted/contacted
- ☐ Religious and spiritual
- ☐ Had a close encounter when outside
- ☐ You were visited, not taken
- ☐ Have no memory of being in a craft
- ☐ Sense that you will be visited
- ☐ Hear buzzing sounds in head and feel compelled to do something
- ☐ Have visions
- ☐ Receive telepathic messages and downloads of information
- ☐ Have no sensation of electrical tingling
- ☐ Have no marks on body
- ☐ Have no implant
- ☐ Have difficulty sleeping, but don't attribute it to fear of abduction
- ☐ Are happy and stable
- ☐ Have not felt motion in mattress
- ☐ Do not have lighted orbs floating in homes
- ☐ Are not intuitive or psychic
- ☐ Have not been healed and cannot heal others

☐ Have not had a near-death experience
☐ Have no phobias
☐ Had very positive experiences
☐ Have OBEs, channel, or altered state of consciousness
☐ Feel calm and curious about your experiences
☐ Would not end your experiences
☐ This experience has given you a special purpose
☐ Say the ETs are kind, gentle, and friendly
☐ Visited by the Greys, Mantis, kind human types, or Tall Whites
☐ Have a high degree of empathy for others
☐ Have a sense of universal connectedness
☐ Are an empath
☐ Have not sought support

Are you neither? *(Check all that apply.)*

☐ Experiences began as an adult
☐ Taken by gargoyles, evil Reptilians, or amphibians
☐ Not taken by the typical cast of ET entities
☐ Had highly negative experiences
☐ NHI entities are mean or evil
☐ NHI entities sodomize you
☐ NHI entities torture you
☐ NHI entities force you to watch as they kill humans
☐ Have recurring nightmares
☐ Mind seems possessed
☐ Forced to harm others
☐ Taunted
☐ Wake up with blistered skin
☐ Health is failing
☐ Have turned away from religious beliefs
☐ Suffer from chronic pain
☐ Take opioids or abuse alcohol

WHEN YOU DISCOVER THAT IT MAY NOT BE ET: GHOSTS AND PARANORMAL PHENOMENA

Denise Stoner
with Kathleen Marden and Ann Castle

Did you know that UFOs, NHI entities, and paranormal phenomena have a lot in common? They all appear to possess interdimensional properties. UFOs have been observed phasing in and out of view. NHI entities have the ability to pass through solid surfaces and simply show up in the homes of experiencers. And paranormal phenomena have been observed by the vast majority of experiencers. It is no wonder that UFO books are categorized as "Paranormal" in bookstores.

You might be shaking your head and thinking, paranormal means "Not within the range of normal experience or scientifically explainable phenomena."[1] In other words, UFOs are, by definition, part of the paranormal as well. If this thought entered your mind, you are correct. However, UFO researchers believe that UFOs are technologically advanced spacecraft from elsewhere that can be back-engineered when our level of scientific development approaches theirs. Therefore, UFOs can be understood by science. We have metallic fragments, implants with isotopic ratios of meteoric origin, and military gun camera videos of them. There is evidence that the US government has recovered crashed nonterrestrial vehicles.

When it comes to understanding the crew inside the craft, we enter shaky ground. Shall we view them as astronauts from another planet in our galaxy? Are they intelligent robots or cyborgs? Or are they sentient beings from a higher dimension? We know that they phase in and out of our visual range. They can simply appear and disappear on a bluish, rounded, funnel-like tractor beam of some kind. Their technological advancement is obvious, but in some ways, they seem like ghosts.

If you are an experiencer, you have probably observed paranormal phenomena in your home. The most commonly observed phenomena are light orbs, poltergeist activity, shadow people, objects that disappear into the ether and might never return, windows and doors that open and close on their own, bathroom plumbing that operates without human assistance, and appliances that turn off and on. Or you might have sensed that something unseen is walking on your bed. At its height, this activity can be unnerving and disruptive to your emotional well-being and quality of life, but it tends to settle down over time.

As an experiencer of UFO abduction and paranormal activity for more than sixty years, I (Denise) have a long history of coping with these unusual events. Sometimes they have been disruptive in my life. However, I have proactively turned them into an avocation in an attempt to differentiate between the two sources: UFOs and the paranormal. Could two entirely different phenomena exhibit similar characteristics? As I carefully monitored these perplexing events in my own life, I came to this conclusion: "Yes, a few come from the same source, but not enough to establish a definite pattern over time." Once I began to document my experiences and research both sides of the spectrum, my exploration opened the door to a vast new educational highway. It led to proficiency in both the ET and paranormal fields and to the answers I was seeking.

When experiencers believe they are being visited by what could be NHI entities from other planets but suddenly report they are also being visited by the spirit of a great grandmother, it is important to look at the detailed characteristics of each occurrence. Are there lines of demarcation between the two? Are they precisely the same, or are they different?

ORBS

Did you know that the spirit of your great-grandmother, an angel, a demon, or that of an ET might show up in an orb? Using available energy, as visiting spirits seem to do when attempting to show themselves to us, they may manifest as floating heads with the actual features of our late loved ones. These often-colorful round objects appear to have intelligence and might dart here and there or float gently just out of reach.

Orbs are sometimes invisible to the naked eye but show up in digital photographs. Perhaps the light spectrum they emit is outside the range of human vision but is visible to cameras and pets. Or perhaps they are simply particles of dust that appear as orbs in the photographs. Dust orbs have fuzzy outer edges and do not exhibit distinct intelligence. When we see a face in a dust orb, we must consider pareidolia as a possible explanation. Pareidolia will cause the human mind to turn random shadows into human faces, shapes, animals, and the like. This is a common occurrence when we gaze at clouds in the sky and see faces or animals, or when we see Jesus on a piece of toast.

Luminescent orb *(courtesy of Jim S.)*

Kathleen had an unnerving experience with a luminescent orb in 1983, when she and her young children were visiting her mother's home in southern New Hampshire. Here's her story:

> I was fast asleep in what had been my childhood bedroom when I was awakened during the night by a noise emanating from the bedroom next to mine. This room, which had formerly been my brother's bedroom, was fraught with paranormal activity after a UFO had landed across the street on my grandparents' farm.
>
> During my college years, I took my then-boyfriend home one weekend for a family fishing trip. My brother was away in the military service, so my boyfriend stayed in his bedroom. Everyone was fast asleep in the middle of the night, when several coat hangers mysteriously left my brother's closet, traveled across the room, and landed on top of my boyfriend. He ran shrieking from the house and returned

only under the condition that he did not have to reenter the haunted bedroom. (Needless to say, this experience was not conducive to a long-lasting relationship.)

Fourteen years later, my four-year-old son was sleeping in this room. He was a good sleeper who generally slept through the night. But on this night, he was creating a ruckus, shrieking with delight, and running back and forth in this room that had, years before, earned a notorious reputation for paranormal activity. I rose from my bed prepared to scold my son for waking me up in the middle of the night—that is, until my eyes met a truly shocking sight. My young son was wreaking havoc with a white baseball-size luminous orb. It was darting across the room, and he was jumping into the air, delightedly chasing it from location to location. The orb appeared to have intelligence, as it moved whenever my son neared it and seemed to have a blissful energy about it. Needless to say, I was astonished! I had never seen an apparition of this kind. I promptly scooped my young son into my arms and hightailed it back to my bedroom where we spent the night in my bed.

Being a scientifically minded person, I attempted to find a prosaic explanation for the orb. Was it ball lightning? I investigated the weather conditions and discovered that there were no thunderstorms in the area. I tested other hypotheses, but in the end I realized that it could not have been attributable to natural causes. Years later, I received a video of an identical orb from one of the experiencers whose case I was investigating. It slid down his bedroom wall, changed direction, and flew across the room to his prone body. It then hesitated and shot rainbow-colored beams downward before it descended into his body and healed his disease.

Yet, I am not certain that either luminescent orb was ET related or merely a paranormal event. No UFO was observed either time, so we cannot assume that it originated on a UFO.

We can be observant, become proactive, and see what direction these bright lights take. Did the light whiz out a window to a larger object, such as a craft, waiting for it to depart to places unknown? Did it enter through the window ready to expand into a full-size NHI entity, to whisk a child to a waiting craft? Did it disappear down a hallway only to fade from view as if making its way to another realm—one we are not able to see? Did it emit enough light to reflect off walls? Did it sparkle, or was it luminescent? If so, it could hold extraterrestrial intelligence. Luminescent orbs are the most frequently reported paranormal phenomena by NHI entity experiencers. More than 60 percent of the survey takers who participated in MUFON's Experiencer Survey have observed lighted orbs in their homes. If you see one, photograph it if you can, watch it closely, and document its characteristics in your journal. Each and every time you have an unusual experience, your notes and photos will be there to help sort out the details of what has actually occurred.

Over time, many people become less fearful of these orbs when they accept the idea that they are visiting spirits, especially of deceased loved ones. The witness tends to be more willing to observe without hiding in fear, and if future events occur, the witness is often encouraged by family and friends to begin asking questions. In turn, this effort at communication may open something between the visitor and our sensitive or psychic selves, allowing the situation to expand or to use more available energy. This is only one example of how spirits are able to enter our environment.

COLD SPOTS

Many movies and paranormal television shows have mentioned cold spots. Perhaps you have felt a cold spot where the vague form of a spirit has appeared. Spirits need energy to show themselves to us, and they can pull that energy from people, pets, plants, electrical appliances or grids, or other power sources. The spot will be a lower temperature than the surrounding area because the spirit has pulled energy to help it manifest. Spirits can draw energy from electrical devices as well. Investigators who have attempted to capture a form or image near a cold spot have observed their fully charged camera batteries, recording devices, and other devices become totally drained of energy. They may feel chilled as the energy from their bodies is used to assist the spirit to remain in place here on the Earth plane.

Your observation of the deceased person might appear in various forms. At first, the person might be visible in black and white, as if in an old photograph. Next, the person might be in glossy color yet look like a still print. In future visits, the person's visibility may improve more. You might observe the spirit's head or bust appearing, like you would see in a short video where your visitor acknowledges you with a nod of the head or slight smile. Voices or conversations are not heard or exchanged with these types of manifestations because they are weak examples of what a visiting spirit is capable of doing. Perhaps this is only an attempt to give us a glimpse that there is a possible place of existence elsewhere.

MEDIUMSHIP AND CHANNELING

When a human is sensitive or welcomes a visiting spirit, there seems to be permission given from the human side to the spirit side for the visiting spirit to enter our realm. Some humans have the ability to serve as a medium or channel to allow ETs or deceased loved ones to enter their bodies and use their consciousness to communicate with us. Mediumship is the process by which a human allows an entity to enter his or her mind to communicate via words or symbols. The human maintains control of the situation, uses his or her regular voice, and can end the communication at will. Channeling occurs when an entity enters the mind, consciousness, and body of the human and takes control of his or her vocal cords to facilitate communication. Often the demeanor and voice of the human change temporarily, and often the human channel has no memory of the event. We are now learning that channelers may communicate with visiting ETs who can insert their consciousness into the body of the willing human. The human's consciousness steps aside as the ET conveys messages to us. However, some investigators suspect that these are not ETs, only playful human spirits or demons.

Through many professional investigations, it has been discovered that spirit visits escalate once an opening has been created. In these types of physical hauntings where the spirits are aware of the humans and communicate, they seem to discover ways to make use of the available energy. They can become full manifestations of people who once lived on Earth. These full manifestations are very rare and can show up as fuzzy, not completely formed, semi-transparent black-and-white figures. Or they might appear just like a person they once knew who would come through the door after a day at work, toss a hat on the table, and walk through the room as if headed for a snack. The only difference is that, should you follow this spirit into the next room, no one will be there. Perhaps observers will experience fear or the sense of grief they recently went through at a memorial service for a friend or loved one.

This type of experience happened to my mother when my grandfather passed away. She was sitting on the sofa reading, not grieving, when he walked through the front door. While alive, he walked through the door, through the living room, and down the back stairs to his apartment, which was the bottom portion of her parents' duplex. Soon after passing, he would turn on the inside lights and open certain cabinet doors in the kitchen. The family was sure it was him because we caught glimpses of the summer hat he always wore moving through the kitchen. Along with that, the cabinets he opened were the ones in which he kept tiny bottles of scotch whiskey for his one drink the doctor allowed before he turned in for the night. The lights turned on were the ones that led to his bedroom, through the living room to the kitchen. Those lights were often turned off again before dawn, and none of the family did this. Who else could it have been? This behavior continued for two years until the family leased his apartment to a new tenant. We assumed that it stopped because the new occupant said nothing about being disturbed by a ghost!

With these kinds of circumstances, all of us want to use our deductive processes, put on our thinking caps, keep journals, and begin to compare the experiences. We need to be unbiased and report to knowledgeable individuals who will, in turn, go to their experts for additional information.

RESIDUAL HAUNTINGS

How do we separate a residual haunt from one that is not? A residual haunt is also referred to as a stone tapping, because many of these spirits are witnessed walking the tops of stone castles, like soldiers in full military regalia. Or they might linger at old jails, historic homes, or buildings where tragedies once occurred. Time-related incidents somehow record themselves within the walls of a granite structure, where there is a good recording crystal, such as quartz. Add running water as a source of static electricity, which increases Earth's natural ability to make its own type of video recorder, and forever ghosts can be presented. They usually appear predictably, at a certain time of day or a certain day of the month. These figures do not recognize us, nor can we draw their attention to us. They cannot react, change what they are doing, cause us harm, move objects, or change the script they are following. They are not aware of our presence because they do not have consciousness and are, in fact, just recordings of the past.

What can you do when you discover or suspect you are experiencing a visiting spirit? How can you be proactive while waiting for or searching for the right investigative team to help? One important factor that is often forgotten is the need for historic facts that are available not only on the building(s) but also the land and surrounding areas. Was the town involved in any kind of natural or manmade disaster, such as a plant explosion, where there were a significant number of sudden deaths? You can gather information through old newspaper articles and other sources in libraries, churches, and halls of records. Historical societies have volunteers who may be happy to do the research for you. Don't be afraid to tell them you may have a ghost because they have probably heard this explanation before.

Have these historical documents on hand to assist in the investigators' work. You will not only help them but also show your willingness to participate in searching for answers. Neighbors can also be a great source of information if they have lived in the area for some time. Doing your homework will help your efforts in solving this mystery and greatly benefit the team you have asked to help you find answers.

POLTERGEIST ACTIVITY

Another factor to consider is poltergeists. What are they, and where do they come from? Poltergeist activity is caused by psychic effects and is not spirit based. Telekinetic activity is the cause of these activities, and they are generated by an agent or person. Multiple factors combine to make this telekinetic pot come to a boil and then explode with many degrees of energy force, which can build stronger over time.

What might cause poltergeist activity to come into a home, business, or other type of dwelling? Such activity has many causes, such as stress, emotional upheaval, psychological distress, hormonal activity, family dynamics, and more. Individuals who are generating poltergeist activity might have no other method of permanently removing the unpleasant effects or pressure they are feeling. When energy from one or more of the above causes is repressed, it builds up, and like an explosive device, it eventually detonates. Therefore, a psychic release takes place, which often causes total chaos for the family and anyone in the line of observation. We must point out that most activity of this type is short lived, especially if immediate help is sought, through therapists, as long as they are knowledgeable and willing to work with this issue. Depending on the range of power, this type of activity can result in scratches, pinches, slaps, and even bites. Differentiating between this type of activity and the demonic can be extremely difficult and should be left to professionals in the field.

Another experience I (Denise) had would be a good example of how this activity can present itself. At one time, I cared for foster children in my home. One of these was a boy I fostered from the time he was a baby until age six. Here's how I remember my time with him:

He was a sweet baby who smiled all the time and never complained. By the time he was age three, I could see he needed to be busy with activities above his age level, or he would get into mischief, such as painting the beautiful almond-colored carpet in my guest bedroom with my pink blush makeup, gold nail polish, and red lipstick. Those items were in my top dresser drawer, and he obtained them while I was running his bath. He was able to keep them hidden until the following morning when he climbed out of his crib, did his deed, and came through to wake me up just prior to 5:45 a.m.

His expertise in staying one step ahead of me progressed to a level no one could keep up with. My husband and I obtained a therapist and, at her advice, enrolled him in a special child-care group at the YMCA. This group was intended to give him some social experience outside the home, to meet other adults and children, and to learn self-control. He was a very charming and handsome but manipulative child. He was also easily depressed and kept his emotions, such as anger, inside. We were using the 1970s child-rearing recommendations, such as time-out periods and choice options rather than saying "No."

By the time he was four, his behavior had become worse. One day, I was cleaning up one of his disasters, and the only way to keep my sanity was to have him sit down at a table near me. I instructed him not to move. I was standing sideways in order to observe both him and the mess I was cleaning. He was so upset that he put his arms at his side, doubled his fists, and began to fuss quietly to himself. He spoke no words but uttered sounds like a vibrational humming.

Earlier in the day, I had been making a grocery list and doing my nails. On the table sat a pencil, a bottle of nail polish, and a small note pad. Within about three minutes, these items began to roll, on their own, toward the edge of the level table. The note pad slid at a slower pace than the other items. The pencil gained momentum while I stood there dumbstruck and staring. The most amazing thing occurred next. As the pencil fell off the edge, for a brief moment, it hesitated and hovered in midair. This little boy ran to the door, showing shock himself. He left the room just as the rest of the objects plunged to the floor. Once he was gone, the energy that was moving the objects dissipated.

He also was able to scratch or poke other people without touching them. His antics caused my neighbor to become quite fearful of him. The little boy left our home and was not in my family's lives by the time he turned six, so I have no further information on his life or what became of him. When he left, the poltergeist activity ceased.

Some people associate poltergeist activity with the demonic, but there was nothing demonic involved. I was able to determine this child had all the ingredients necessary to create the perfect environment for poltergeists to appear. Had he been an adult, this activity could have been much more forceful and possibly much more difficult to sort out.

(Refer to Chapter 9 for information on telekinesis.)

OBJECT ATTACHMENTS

Do spirits from the past become attached to objects they once owned? Absolutely! This spirit attachment can become greatly confusing to the new owner due to the type of object, where it came from, the land location, building, and the previous owner. If you feel you have a visiting spirit or activity due to a new object brought into your home, there are ways to investigate.

Begin by narrowing the field. What was the date and time the suspected object entered the home? Where is the object located in the home? Is the activity positive, negative, or mischievous? Can you guess whether this might be male or female activity? Which gender might have owned the object? What type of emotion might this object have created in the previous owner, if any? Don't look for an attachment to each and every item you purchase from an antique store or estate sale. You just never know when one will appear.

My husband and I had an extraordinary experience with new furniture we purchased. Here is our story:

> My husband and I (Denise) were looking for new dining room and bedroom furniture a few years ago. We were in no hurry until I finally spotted a sale on a bedroom set that included a triple dresser, armoire, and nightstands. We could not beat the price, and everything matched, unlike our collection of mishmash in the room at the time. Then we went on a search for the dining room set. Shortly following that purchase, I spotted the same brand as our bedroom furniture, in one of the big box department stores, at an amazing price. We went down and purchased a table with inserts and eight chairs. After we had the furniture for eight months, the paranormal activity commenced.
>
> Once the activity began, we did some research and learned that it could be related to the wood and where it came from. Both sets were beautifully carved Caribbean hardwood that came from a plantation in one particular area of a Caribbean island.
>
> We tend to use our table as a work space when we are not eating, so mail sat there ready to go out or to sort. We had recently lost a family member and had to sign an important document for the lawyer. Once the paperwork was signed,

we placed the stamped envelope on the table ready to send out on the next business day. In the morning, we walked to the table to pick up the envelope and it was not there. We looked everywhere for the envelope. We were certain it was on the table, but it was not there. Nor was it on the floor, the chairs, or any of the counters. This item was not to be found. We had to request another copy be sent to us overnight. It was never placed on the table, due to the need for quick response, and this time we were able to mail it.

Another time, I was suddenly missing a necklace I had placed on the table while I dressed for a night out. There was a large mirror on the wall next to the table that I used when I put on my jewelry. As I returned to the dining room to pick up my necklace and place it around my neck, it was no longer there. Another search left me empty handed.

That night while in bed contemplating the now two missing items in less than five weeks, I glanced up at the bedroom doorway. Drifting across rather quickly was the dark silhouette of a woman in a gown that would fit the *Gone with the Wind* antebellum period. She was wearing a bonnet, but her long hair flowed out from under it, down her back. She did not look my way and was floating quickly as if on a mission. I could not see through her but only caught a quick glimpse as she passed through our dark living room. I always have our TV on in the bedroom, so it gives some light to the outer room although it is around a corner. There was no doubt in my mind that I had seen this female figure. I was wide awake. I still did not connect this female with our tropically designed table.

Some time passed until one of us placed another item on the table and it went missing. I began to make a connection and decided to test my suspicion. We decided to give our spirit a name and dubbed her "Lady of the Table." We have seen her a few times, but she never looks back at us. She is always dressed in the same lacy plantation garb, with gloves. Her goal is to reach the table, pause long enough to see if there is an item of interest, and carry it into the ether where it remains hidden.

We have asked to have our items returned, but only one was found at a much later date. That was the first missing document. We discovered it under the seat of our car. When we made a quick stop, it slid out from under the seat and landed at my husband's feet, which was a total surprise to us. The rest has never been found or returned. We have learned a wise lesson: never place anything that resembles a document requiring a signature or jewelry that sparkles—whether real stones or not—on or near that table. Again, I must say, this is not the typical haunted object where the spirit involved is ever seen, only the energy from it is noticed, and the exercise of sorting it out begins.

SPIRIT VISITATION

At times, the visit from a loved one can occur when the bond was close and special between two people. I changed the following story slightly in order to protect the individual who told me about it because I can no longer obtain permission to write it.

At least eight years ago, a person in my life talked about the ability to predict some future events with some accuracy and also had some visits from relatives who had passed on. Only the two individuals knew of this nightly practice until I was told, many years later, that it was still ongoing. My friend was in bed a few nights after her spouse passed, but was not asleep, when suddenly a picture frame floated in front of her wall. Inside that frame was the face of her newly departed spouse. His framed face had a calm, serene look about it, and a feeling of peace fell over my friend. After several nights of this activity, the frame did not appear again. However, she noticed a gentle rustling of her sheets that became a nightly practice of tucking the covers under her chin. It appears that the one still living on our earthly plane was shown affection despite what we call "physical death." I believe this was a sign that life exists after death, and if we pay attention, spirits can communicate in special ways to comfort us in our grief and also to let us know they still remain near, just out of sight from human eyes.

Be ever so cautious of what you wish for though . . . you just might get it. I used to hold a class in meditation, and eight of us became close regulars. All were fascinated in psychically reading future events and receiving possible weather activity for Florida, such as hurricanes that might approach our coast, which coast, and so on. We did readings for each other by offering a question prior to sitting in meditation. Then we collected the impressions we received at the end of the meditation. We became very good at it, and several people regularly matched each other's answers, wrote them down, and handed them to me for proof.

There happened to be an old cemetery directly behind the place where we held our weekly meditation, and it had been unkempt for years. None of us even thought about it until one night when we decided to ask if, during meditation, we could receive information from one of the individuals who had been buried in the cemetery. We always lit a white candle, said a healing prayer, closed in tight to each other in a circle, and waited for darkness to settle in.

This was the front room of a shop owned by one of the participants. There was a front door to the street and a back room holding a refrigerator for food and other storage. Parking was directly in front. Settled in, we asked for a message and turned on our CD of quiet music. We were all accustomed to entering into a deep meditative state lasting for a solid hour and twenty minutes. The last twenty minutes were for us to begin to "awaken" and come back to the room to discuss our experiences, plus share the messages or information we received.

About twenty minutes prior to the end of our meditation, a loud bang brought us totally out of our meditative state. What appeared to be a very strong spirit blew out the candle and turned on the snowy screen of a TV set that was mounted on the wall. Eyes as big as dinner plates, mouths hanging open, we looked around expecting damage of some kind. We heard footsteps in the doorway to the storage room and in walked a tall, thin figure wearing a tall top hat, coat with tails, tall black shoes, striped vest, and he had a very serious round face, with an almost marching gait. He walked through the people closest to the door, causing quite a cool wind as he entered the center of the circle. He stood there fading in and out like a bad TV picture before walking out through the glass in the front door. The TV snow turned off, and there we sat in the pitch dark with only a street light on in the distance and a few cars passing on the road.

We did not have much to say until we ended the meditation and went to a restaurant for coffee and a meal. Then we all began talking at once. This visitation became the topic of discussion for years when we got together. We suspected that this gentleman visitor might have heard our request and paid a visit to let us know he was still around somewhere in the ether. This experience is still as clear to me today as it was many years ago.

Most of these visitors are not earthbound or stuck here without choice. They can come and go at will and are just visitors in a place they used to live, were comfortable in, and perhaps enjoyed. Some were hooked on earthly addictive goodies such as alcohol, tobacco, food, and sparkly things, and they resist the calling of their guardian spirit to leave behind earthly possessions. There are many reasons a spirit might remain earthbound. Deceased children might not know what to do or where to go if they lost their parents in the turmoil of a tragedy, so they stay thinking they can reunite with Mom or Dad. I could go on and on with the many scenarios discovered throughout history, but it is not necessary for the information I am sharing here.

I have explained the many ways ghosts, spirits, and the unseen can show themselves to us. Personally, I have drawn a line of distinction between my paranormal events and the ETs that have been in my life since I was a young child.

Many experiencers believe there is a strong link between the paranormal and UFO activity. Shadow people, light orbs in their homes, and poltergeist activity seem somehow related to their personal relationship with the nonhuman entities who whisk them away to an alien environment. Many experiencers lose property as if it had disappeared into the ether.

In one case, a Texas woman discovered that her driver's license that had been tightly lodged in her wallet had simply vanished. When an extensive search failed to locate her license, she replaced it. She then moved three times to two different states. Each time she moved, she replaced her license with a new one and turned in her old license. Twenty-five years later, she took her car to a garage to be serviced. When she returned to her residence, she opened the garage door and pulled her car into its resting spot. This is when she noticed something lying on the garage floor. Curious, she picked it up, and to her amazement it was the driver's license she had lost twenty-five years earlier! Had it disappeared into the ether? Did she have an interdimensional portal? Wouldn't it be interesting to know for certain?

The investigation of these activities is of vital importance if we are to gain an understanding of the true nature of these events. Are they related to contact by extraterrestrial beings, or are they caused by visitors from interdimensional realms on our own planet? There are many options for capturing evidence, sorting it out, and deciding what the best course of action might be. (See Chapter 3 for additional suggestions on how to investigate your experiences.) You will be introduced to additional thoughts and information when you read the next chapter.

CHAPTER 6 CHECKLIST: SORTING OUT SPIRIT ACTIVITY FROM NHI ENTITY ACTIVITY

- Keep a journal in a handy place and document your observations immediately.
- Record all of the details pertaining to your observation.
- Act like a scientist and never jump to fast conclusions.
- Learn more about the characteristics of paranormal activity. Who is removing the top from your ketchup bottle? Was it a family member, a spirit, or an NHI entity?
- What color was the orb you observed? Did you see anything or anyone inside this orb?
- How did this orb behave? Did it seem to have intelligence? Did it interact with you or a family member?
- When did your paranormal activity begin? Was it after a UFO abduction? Was it after you purchased an antique or occult memorabilia? Or has it always been part of your life?
- Did your paranormal experiences begin when you moved into a new home?
- Did it begin when your child was going through puberty? When you were in turmoil?
- Does it occur on a regular basis or within days of your UFO contact event?

Chapter 7

ANGELS, DEMONS, AND PARASITES: DO THESE ENTITIES EXIST?

Denise Stoner
with Kathleen Marden and Ann Castle

Angels, demons, and parasites—yes, these entities *do* exist! There are many, showing themselves to humans in a multitude of signs, forms, shapes, and more. Even what is written here is not enough to explain the unbelievable number of different types of entities that exist in our world, and not only show themselves to us but also demonstrate their abilities by making use of available human energy. I (Denise) have been working with the paranormal, including the negative aspects of it, for forty years. In this chapter, I give several examples that will send perfect visual pictures to your brain, making it clear what you need to look for, listen for, and think about when deciding whether or not you are dealing with negative entities.

These negative entities are aware of our every emotion and when to take advantage of an opening left by even a slightly negative factor spotted in our being. Although negativity is dark, it shines like a beacon to them, guiding the negative force toward a dark place inside of us at any moment. There appears to be a recipe that, under a certain set of circumstances, can either invite positive angels or negative entities into our lives. These include the full spectrum from naughty spirits all the way to attachments that do just that—attach to humans until they are removed and sent away. The worst entity is the demon who possesses!

The least powerful of these entities are parasites. First, parasites are energetic beings that can be from Earth, the astral plane, or another dimension; or they can even appear as ETs. They have a lower level of consciousness and can be automatic and animalistic in their actions. Like amoebas, they feed, react, and feed again. Parasites can deplete our energy because they feed off the actual life force from our energetic body. As a result, we feel tired and irritable, which brings on more emotional problems over time and finally can cause physical problems.

Attachments have individual consciousness and intelligence. Like parasites, they are energetic beings that can be from Earth, the astral plane, or another dimension. Some are even the spirits of deceased humans that do not want to move on to the next realm. Others are deceased loved ones who erroneously believe they can help us by attaching to us, but often they transfer to us the negative physical symptoms that caused their death.

The worst of the negative entities, demons, are from the Satanic realm and can use us to commit evils acts. They are the most cunning. Demons can enter by first convincing us that we are here to serve some special purpose or as special soldiers. They are tricksters and will draw us into their web to control our ability to make positive decisions on our own.

Let's begin with why negative entities enter lives and bring complications into the presence of human beings who are unprepared for the total wreck their lives can become. Lives already in turmoil become more disturbed, and loss of control is imminent if the early warning signs are ignored. Negative parasitic entities and attachments feed on human energy and can treat us like batteries, using our energy to survive! They are attracted to weakened auras (refer to Chapter 9 for more information on auras) and strong negative emotions, such as hopelessness, fear, and loathing. Some negative entities latch on to the place we are most vulnerable or find a place within the dwelling where they sit and wait for an opportunity to show themselves. The demonic entities also use human energy but want us to commit evil acts.

There are a multitude of reports of demons, possessions, exorcisms, and evil taking over in the worst possible way! Minds are fooled into thinking they are consumed by these forces and are beyond human control. Usually, proper investigations are not done, or if they are carried out, they exclude whether there has been a true invasion of a place, person, or thing by something evil. Many factors are involved, including the person's mental state, how that person might feel about the situation, what he or she believes, and how it is all handled during stress. Three basic steps culminate in a full-blown possession of a person: *depression, oppression,* and finally, *possession.*

HOW DOES THIS BEGIN, AND WHAT DO WE LOOK FOR?

The first condition, *depression,* involves feeling extremely sad or despondent with an inability to concentrate. Insomnia and feelings of sadness become more extreme for no apparent reason. In addition, feelings of dejection and hopelessness linger with no reasonable explanation for some length of time.

The second condition, *oppression,* increases the chances of parasitic attachment—because even more power is lost. Oppressed victims have moved from *depressed* to *oppressed,* which means they are hampered with constant grief and a sense of failure, and they believe they have a heavy burden at work and/or at home. They are totally downtrodden, maltreated, and helpless, and they sense there is no way out. Having a discussion with these oppressed people is almost impossible. Sleep deprivation is common, and if you come face to face with these individuals, you will discover eye contact is impossible. They feel as if something else is controlling them at times, thinking is impossible, and their decision-making process is out of control. Since they feel powerless, the parasite now jumps at the opportunity!

Knowledgeable outside observers begin to wonder if there is a personality disorder, but because there is so little conversation, they are left not knowing what to think. Oppressed people withdraw socially, needing to keep all their feelings internalized. Since there appears to be no way out, they sink deeper into the hole. These negative beings have their tentacles attached to these people with no intention of letting go, until they feel there is a better source of energy to draw from, or the tormented individuals obtain the proper help. However, the afflicted people's downtrodden emotional state works to the evil entities' advantage, allowing them to strengthen and gain power.

The worst types of entities are *demons.* Every few years, books, movies, TV shows, and lectures on demons spike public interest. Media hype sells news, books, and movies. Some believe that our obsession with demons, through the media and negative human emotions, can increase their power and malevolence. Demonic worship might increase but be countered by a spike in religious faith.

In work I have done on the paranormal (especially in Denver, Colorado), I have witnessed only a couple of people with an attachment but no possession. Since moving to Florida in 1985, I believe that something has changed. It may have to do with a change in the vibrational field or the way people are feeling as a whole. I have seen at least four people I would consider possessed, and I've lost count

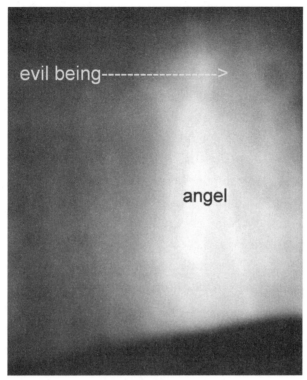

Matt's photo *(courtesy of MUFON)*

of those who have parasites. However, this is still not an immense number overall.

What characterizes a person possessed by a demon? A demon has *dominion* over or exclusive control over a person's soul and behavior. The person can speak in a different voice, reject religion, and swear when he or she did not do so previously. This individual also exhibits feelings of pain at the sight of a religious object (especially a cross) and emits sounds of pain when splashed with holy water or touched with a cross. If touched on the forehead with a cross, the person's skin may burn and blister, and screams can be heard coming from deep in the throat. This person can make threats, growl, or even display telekinetic ability on religious items.

Unlike parasites, demons can harm a person, such as making deep scratches in groups of three that suddenly appear on the person's body. These marks are made just to demonstrate their strength, so others can witness their presence and control. Mentioning a religious figure such as Jesus, reading from the Holy Bible in the presence of a demon, or repeating the exorcist's prayer will greatly anger the demon. The possessed person often exhibits a change in personality that is mostly negative, frightening, and sometimes violent. Should this person attempt to fight the demon, there may be loud banging, disconnected voices, objects thrown, scratches on the victim's body, and more.

Sometimes, demons leave odors of rotting flesh or sulfur. The corners of a room may stink, and then the smell is gone. Certain rooms may be infested with flies, maggots, or other insects, such as cockroaches, where there was no infestation before, even if the room has no plumbing or other opening to the outside. This scenario is the worst of the worst, possibly the rarest, and requires the help of a trained exorcist.

Unless you have a trained exorcist to remove the demon, you will probably lose the battle because the demon will war against you. Then the demon will be stronger in its determination to show the power it has over the victim and all who dared confront it. *No one—I repeat—no one should endeavor to use the Exorcist's Prayer in order to expel a demon from a person.* This prayer is meant for the exclusive use of a priest trained in the *Rite of Exorcism*. If it is used by anyone else, the results could affect everyone involved in a very negative way. Also, no one should consider taking a course online that will issue you a certificate as a "certified exorcist." This certificate has no real value.

I agree that there are successful Native American shamans, ordained ministers, and so on, but very few others have also been trained in exorcism. Just running through a ritual with no power behind it gives no results and only leaves an angry victim. If nothing else, heed my warning that you should not attempt an exorcism.

The following account describes the first time I recognized a true possession. To ensure anonymity, I have protected the person's true identity. The possessed man, in his early sixties, was diagnosed with a disease supposedly in its late stages. He had many medical issues throughout the years but chose not to take advice from several medical doctors. His choices resulted in various medical crises. Each episode gave him the attention of close friends and family members. They cared for him so well that he did not find it necessary to recover fully and begin self-care. He was demanding, angry, accusatory, and abusive. No one could please him. This behavior continued for years, and often a new illness would be added. Some were real, but others were not fully diagnosed or couldn't be verified.

Doctors prescribed medications causing reactions that did not endanger the person's life but had an odd range of side effects that the man used to gain even more attention. Several times he should have died, and once while on the brink of death, he suddenly recovered in a matter of two hours. Doctors declared this a medical mystery.

Just as a physician was about to fit a piece of the puzzle into place and solve some of the mystery, the patient would fire that physician. Two family members had figured out his game, and they were soon ousted from the intimate circle. He demanded complete loyalty, so no one was permitted to speak to these family members! Finally, another family member reported these dysfunctional and disturbing medical issues to one of the physicians hoping to help the man. At this point, there was no suspicion of demonic involvement because the people involved never thought to add that possibility to the ever-evolving abnormal transformations.

Years later, when the man was once again in the hospital, I received a call from one of his close relatives, asking me for a visit and informing me the patient now had congestive heart failure and was expected to die within twelve hours. The family might have to decide whether to remove life support. At the hospital, I discovered special equipment just outside the patient's room that monitored the heart and other organs. I inquired as to the man's condition, and the situation regarding removing his life support, as told to me earlier, was repeated and therefore confirmed.

I did not know what my own feelings would be because I, too, had a relationship with this individual. Even though I had experience with dying people, I found it necessary to remain at a distance, to observe from my decided point of reference. It somehow felt strange and unreal, but I didn't know what *that* meant. I had never experienced difficulty approaching a dying person or holding his or her hand, speaking softly . . . knowing what to do. This situation was different. I moved forward cautiously until I was halfway between the window and his bedside. At that moment, I suddenly realized I hadn't really looked at this man in the bed. I knew that I was so wrapped up in my senses that I did not hear a sound—not the hiss of oxygen or the click of the heart and oxygen monitors.

I then began to pay attention to the sounds and the completely still body that lay in the hospital bed. I noticed his head, which appeared to be considerably larger than usual. I reasoned he may have fluid collecting there. Then I realized his double chin must have developed five layers since I last saw him only five days earlier. So, there were some oddities I blamed on the heart difficulties. Then I noticed his breathing was the most guttural, labored drawing of breath I had ever heard, and I know what a death rattle is. Intuitively, I knew something wasn't right but had no idea what.

Then, for no reason, fear began creeping into my body. I told myself that I was being foolish and to ground myself. The man on the bed now lifted his head and rambled a few sentences that made no sense at all. I did not recognize a word and, stupidly, asked him to repeat himself. Into my head came the words, "You missed it. Too bad." I started to feel the atmosphere in the room changing. It seemed to *thicken,* and I began to feel ill. My own death came to mind, and I thought I was going to drop to the floor without being able to call the nurse, who was just outside the door. Before I could think about my next step, I realized the dense air had become like wet cement that seemed to fill the room past my knees. I made the decision to leave quickly and not call for help. This whole line of thinking was insane, and I felt like an actor in some sci-fi movie. For the first time in my life, I was virtually frozen with fear.

Finally, using all my energy, I began the arduous process of leaving that room. I shuffled to the side of the bed because I could not lift my legs out of the thick cement. I leaned over the man and whispered that I would visit again, would say a prayer for him, and was going to leave. As I neared the door, the patient opened his mouth larger than normal, and a hideous growl came out like I had never heard before. At that moment, I knew this was some sort of evil spirit, and I wondered if he had picked it up in the hospital. I had not begun to connect all the past events with this one. I also feared this wicked spirit was after me and wanted to get out of there, although I had only been there for ten minutes.

Using every last ounce of my strength, I dragged myself out the door, and feeling terribly ill, I walked down the hallway hoping I would not end up a patient in the emergency room. I took the elevator to the lobby but did not feel released from the oppressive evil until I was off the elevator and in the entrance. I had to figure out how to deal with this type of entity, so I vowed to learn all I could from that day forward!

However, there is a more. On the way home from the hospital, I phoned the family member with whom I had a very close relationship. He told me that he had stopped by ten minutes before I had to visit the man on his way to work at another hospital. He had experienced this oppressive negativity that I described but left before it got too bad. He stressed that he did not want to go back again, yet he was expected to show up in the morning to make the decision whether or not to have the life support removed. He did not believe he could go back into the room, nor did he have any idea how to explain why.

What happened next is beyond any reasonable explanation, and the nurses should have acknowledged that something was very abnormal. I arrived home around four in the afternoon, had an early dinner, and prepared to spend the evening reading a new book. Around five thirty the phone rang, and the caller identified herself as the nurse taking care of the man. What she told me I recall exactly, as it was short: "Someone here would like to talk to you." My immediate thought was that one of the family members had called me, but that made no sense because they could have called me without assistance. Then a perfectly normal, happy, healthy-sounding voice said, "Hi." It was the man dying of congestive heart failure—the man I had visited and left only two hours previously—the one who made me feel as if I was going to die before I could escape the evil presence.

I had to ask, "Who is this?" The response was absolutely insane! This person invited me to join him at a restaurant for lobster tail when he went home the next day. What? He was back in his own home within a few hours after this event.

From then on, I became hypervigilant. I studied. I spoke to priests who had studied demonic possession. I spoke to anyone who had been involved in the process of understanding how to differentiate demons from visiting family spirits, earthbound spirits, parasites, attachments, and the actual demon who possesses. I wanted to investigate actual cases, research, study, and gain as much knowledge as possible.

As the years passed, this man, much to my sadness, was consumed by this evil. I witnessed a deeply angered, loud-voiced entity, and a female caretaker who threatened those who denied what *IT* demanded. Money was spent that should not have been spent, depleting an elderly person's retirement funds. Huge beetles invaded his room, and banging sounds and other noises tormented anyone in the home. Fires were set but were quickly extinguished. Areas of the home where there are no water lines were flooded. And black mold grew invasively on closet walls. I am sorry to say this man was never helped. He went to his death defeated by the malevolence that consumed his life.

Another incident was related to me by Mady Tobias, the author of Chapter 8. For many years, Mady was a nurse psychotherapist who helped people who had been drawn into and later departed from cults. This is not an account of her work with former cult members, but it is about a young pyromaniac.

The exorcist Malachi Martin asked Mady to evaluate an eleven-year-old boy who set fire to his house. The prescribed procedure preceding an exorcism was a psychological evaluation to rule out mental illness. Martin explained that it was important for her to see this child. His mother brought the boy to Mady's office, and he looked like any other kid his age, neatly dressed and self-confident. When asked why he wanted to set fire to the house, without any hesitation, he looked Mady straight in the eye and described how he planned to kill his parents and brother.

One evening, the boy assembled all the fire supplies and waited until the family was asleep. He then started the fire and fled from the house so he wouldn't be trapped inside. However, the fire awoke the family and they escaped. The boy related his story with a straight face and no emotion of any kind. At the end of the story, he smiled and the pupils of his eyes changed into horizontal slits, like a goat's, not a reptile's or a cat's! Mady ended the interview and recounted the boy's session to Malachi Martin, who apparently wanted her to eliminate a psychiatric diagnosis before he treated the boy for demonic possession. In this case, an exorcism was carried out and the child recovered.

WHEN ALIEN ABDUCTION TURNS OUT TO BE SOMETHING ELSE

My coauthors and I have investigated several suspected alien abduction cases that did not have the markers of UFO abduction. In each case, the experiencers were middle-aged when they had their first experience, which is uncommon among abductees. In some cases, they had made a concerted effort to make contact with advanced NHI entities and initially thought that their attempts had been successful. In others, they had chosen a lover who had an entity attachment. All bore marks on their bodies that were not consistent with the indicators of UFO abduction. There were no scoop marks, grid marks, or cored-out triangles. Nor were there markings that fluoresced under a UV light. There were no medical procedures carried out by NHI entities. These unfortunate individuals were tormented on a nightly basis, often waking up with deep scratches and bite marks on their bodies. They described their abductors as evil, malicious, or highly negative and could not make the malevolence that was afflicting them cease.

In one case, a man had invited contact with NHI entities and was pleased when his attempts were successful. He soon realized, however, that he had called in something that he had not bargained for. Over the ensuing weeks and months, he began to observe a personality change in his once virtuous Christian wife's behavior. Although she had previously been subdued and respectful, her language was now peppered with a level of profanity that would curl any decent person's hair. Her behavior took on a debased sexual acting out, and she became violent, especially toward her husband. The marriage ended after she attempted to run him down with her car.

Now alone, he had to contend with the presence of malevolent entities in his own life. One night, while lying in bed, he sensed a stinging sensation across his back. He walked to his bathroom mirror and observed long welts seared into his flesh by some unknown, invisible force. He sensed an evil presence that he believed was an unseen UFO entity. He began to believe these beings were not technologically advanced extraterrestrials, but demonic entities wreaking havoc on his life. When his oppressor became fully visible, it did not resemble any of the well-known UFO entities that he was aware of. It could appear, disappear, and shapeshift into different forms and seemed to thrive on the terror it inflicted. Over time, malignant oppression destroyed the victim's health. Whenever he fell asleep, he was afflicted by terrifying nightmares of being taken to an alien environment and tortured.

He became a born-again Christian and sought assistance from his minister, but these actions did not end his plight. His search only created greater loathing inside of him. His behavior spiraled downward, causing estrangement from the family he had depended on for moral support. He suffered from a variety of new illnesses that constantly plagued him. No UFO investigator could alleviate this wretched man's suffering. Only a person capable of carrying out an exorcism could have helped this man, but he was resistant to offers of intervention.

In another case, a middle-aged man began dating a new woman. She claimed to be an abductee, and he had an interest in UFOs, so they seemed to share common interests. As their relationship progressed, he began to experience missing time and awakened with burns on his body. She found deep scratches on her back that neither he nor she could have inflicted. They could think of no logical explanation for what caused them. They began to remember being in an alien environment where they were forced to engage in sexual relations with Reptilian entities. Over time, his mood changed, and he became dark and depressed and felt a compulsion to inflict harm upon others. His life spiraled downward as the troubling events progressed. Finally, his life became unbearable, so thinking that he was being taken by Reptilians of extraterrestrial origin, he sought assistance from UFO and paranormal investigators. No one could offer a solution to his suffering. After much agony, he found a Christian group that performed exorcisms. They successfully removed the demonic interdimensional Reptilian shapeshifter that had attached itself to him. Finally, his life was worth living again.

Two women have sent Kathleen photos of blistering burns on their bodies. One had awakened with a sense that she was being strangled and fought off the wolfman who inflicted harm upon her. The other had been beaten over her entire body. Both believed their wounds had been inflicted by extraterrestrials. But why would technologically advanced beings cross the vast expanse of space to inflict pain on humans? Why would they attach themselves to people and torture them on a frequent basis? Why would highly evolved spirits force humans to have sex with them? Why will the rights of exorcism cause these horrific experiences to end? The logical answer to this question is that these abusers are not extraterrestrials. They are shapeshifting demonic entities who prey on those who unwittingly invite them into their lives. Real extraterrestrials do not behave like demons.

ANGELS

The opposite of these evil beings are the angels. To simplify your understanding of angels, here is the theological story. Angels sit at the foot of God, the Source, the Creator, or whatever you consider to be the ALL THAT IS, the great I AM. They serve this powerful consciousness and stand between this Source and humans. They serve the greater good, have performed great miracles, and have saved lives by "being there." For example, say a young child is saved as he or she falls from a tree. Later, the child describes a beautiful gossamer-winged creature who set him or her gently upon the ground. Others speak of mysterious individuals who show up during times of crises. For example, a couple was caught in a raging blizzard when their car broke down. They set out walking to find shelter but were on the brink of losing hope when a stranger came to guide them to safety.

These beings have never resided on Earth, and they have been blessed with power above and beyond what any other has, aside from God. We, as humans, have no power over them and cannot request anything from them except through prayer.

Religious doctrine speaks of other angels—the dark ones or fallen angels—who once sat at the throne of God. The divine consciousness originally gifted all the angels with the same power and does not take gifts away. When the dark angels fell, they took their power with them and could use it against the good, for negative purposes, so we are expected to rise above that negativity. We strive to increase our own elevated level of consciousness and stand against immoral behavior.

Many people who have had near-death experiences or who have been hospitalized describe meeting angels. These heavenly creatures came to comfort, offer healing, and at times guide a person toward the light of the afterlife. Entire books have been written about these experiences.

It would take an entire book to write about angels and their history up to now. Many more people are blessed by the good ones than those who have to deal with the bad.

One last thought that I feel compelled to pass on is the idea that ETs may also be present when humans are in a life-or-death situation. They have appeared disguised as nurses, rescuers, and so on. People have caught glimpses of these ETs and recognized those huge eyes looking down on them out of half-human faces—gentle faces communicating telepathically that they are going to be all right and not to worry. These people survive impossible illnesses or dire situations and live to tell others that an angel with big eyes and telepathy saved their lives.

When I was a young woman, I had a personal experience with one of these benevolent nonhuman entities that I want to share with you. My family had been informed that they should prepare themselves for my impending death. I had almost no chance of surviving a stroke and sepsis. On my deathbed, I looked into the eyes of an ET, who may also have been an angel, and a miracle occurred. I was sent back to complete my mission on Earth and lived to tell my story. This is just another piece of the huge, universal puzzle to ponder.

Some experiencers believe they have been contacted by highly spiritual extraterrestrial entities. These beautiful beings in human form come to their aid whenever they face a personal crisis. They appear out of the ether to impart loving guidance and offer pearls of wisdom to enhance the lives of the humans they visit. They do not behave in the manner of scientists, but as emissaries of love and good will. The individuals whose lives they touch feel as though they have been caressed by an angel. Perhaps they have.

CHAPTER 7 QUESTIONNAIRE: SIGNS OF DEMONIC AND ANGELIC INVOLVEMENT

Complete the following twenty questions. If you answer "yes" to any five of the first ten questions, you might have a negative or demonic entity attachment. If you answer "yes" to any five of the last ten questions, you might have a guardian angel.

Negative

1. Do you experience bad luck or a feeling of loathing whenever you attend a religious service?
2. Are you being taunted by some unknown force?
3. Have you been suspended upside down by your ankles?
4. Have you found deep scratches on your body and have no viable common explanation for what caused them?
5. Are these entities forcing you to harm others?
6. Have you undergone a negative personality change?
7. Are you depressed or in chronic pain?
8. Are the NHI entities in your life shapeshifting Reptilians, gargoyles, or wolf-faced humanoids?
9. Have goat-faced gray orbs been seen on your property?
10. Have you observed a scratch being carved into your skin by an unseen source?

CONTINUES

Positive/Angelic

1. Have you been visited by a kind, loving NHI entity of human appearance?

2. Does this NHI entity comfort you when you feel ill or when you are experiencing emotional pain?

3. Does the NHI entity assist you when you have to make difficult decisions?

4. Have you been delayed when in transit and then discovered that you could have been involved in a fatal accident if you had been on time?

5. Have you found white feathers in your home?

6. Have you been in a terrible accident but walked away without a scratch?

7. Have you seen light beings?

8. Have you witnessed beautiful shimmering lights or flashes of color?

9. Have you experienced a wonderful tingling sensation in your head or body, especially when you are prayerful?

10. Do you have a repetition of the same thing playing over and over in your head?

Chapter 8

HOW TO COPE WITH CONTACT BY NONHUMAN ENTITIES

Madeleine Tobias

In the previous chapters we explored a variety of experiences that involve abductions, communication with NHI entities, paranormal occurrences, and demonic encounters. These events challenge our understanding of ourselves and the world: What is real and what is not? What is inside of us and what is outside? What is next to come?

Let's begin by looking at how we identify ourselves. Who and what am I? What did you believe about yourself and the world when you were growing up? Our sense of self begins to develop very early in childhood as we separate in infancy from our mothers. We are taught about life, first at home, then in school, perhaps in church or synagogue, and by our friends. Who and what we are forms over time from these experiences. Our beliefs about ourselves and the world determine how we behave and how we interact with others; they also form our desires, hopes, and fears. Very simply, what we believe (how we think) affects how we feel (our emotions) and how we behave.

Our desire to fit in with society, beginning with our family and friends at school, supports a conformity to their norms and values.

When I learned to read, at age five or six, I discovered, with a bit of shock, that the words in the book meant someone else had thoughts too! I realized that what *I* think, inside *my* head, is unknown and possibly very different from what others think. Or maybe not.

CONSCIOUSNESS

As a psychotherapist a few decades later, I approached each client as a detective: what makes that person think, feel, and behave the way he or she does? In the early 1980s when I started practicing (incidentally, an accurate word!) psychotherapy, I then used the tools that I had to help clients overcome whatever difficulty they were experiencing. Initially, I utilized a form of therapy that was psychodynamic in origin, based on the work of Sigmund Freud at the turn of the 20th century. This therapy posited that there were three levels of consciousness.

The conscious self is aware of what is happening when awake and could focus one's five senses of sight, sound, smell, hearing, and touch at will. Incidentally, in the 21st century, a few more senses have been discovered, though they are not commonly known. They are "the ability to detect other stimuli beyond these sensory modalities including temperature (thermoception); kinesthetic sense (proprioception); pain (nociception); balance (equilibrioception); and vibration (mechanoreception).[1] I discuss these senses later in the chapter.

The preconscious, or subconscious, is a part of memory that could be brought to awareness by triggers in the environment or by conscious effort to remember. The unconscious is unavailable to the waking mind but could be accessed through dreams. Uncovering the unconscious, as well as the preconscious, was an important aspect to solving a patient's presenting difficulties, according to Freud. This task often involved many years of intensive psychoanalysis with the patient spending three to four days a week on the couch!

Leaving psychodynamic psychotherapy behind (like Freud's belief in the use of cocaine), I then used a brief form of cognitive behavioral therapy to help those with post-traumatic stress disorder. This therapy is based on the belief that emotions such as anger, sadness, fear, and happiness arise from our thoughts or beliefs and then lead to a behavioral response.

So how does this technique help the experiencer understand and deal with abductions and a variety of paranormal happenings? Not much, unless both client and therapist broaden their beliefs about the underlying basis of how our world and consciousness work. I go back to the different kinds of therapy that might be helpful to the experiencer later in this chapter.

In the nuts-and-bolts world we live in, many, if not most people, have difficulty believing in things that cannot be scientifically verified. Even after seventy years of monitoring UFO activity, their existence is not proven to a high percentage of scientists, though a large percentage of the population at large are less skeptical. Those who report abductions (experiencers) commonly report telepathic communication with NHI entities, report becoming more psychic, and describe seeing ETs coming and going through walls and being transported either bodily or astrally to ships. How can we begin to explain this?

Consciousness, as defined by the *Merriam-Webster Dictionary*, is

1. the quality or state of being aware especially of something within oneself
2. the state or fact of being conscious/aware of an external object, state or fact
3. the upper level of mental life of which the person is aware as contrasted with unconscious processes[2]

The preceding definition describes only two states of consciousness. There are many more. The one we are most familiar with is the waking state of consciousness. Our senses are, more or less, alert to what we see, hear, physically feel (such as cold, warmth, touch), smell, and taste. We can also sense temperature, pain, hunger, and thirst. In an altered state of consciousness, some or all of these senses can be blocked or changed. Put us in front of a good movie or great book, and our focus narrows to what is most interesting. Other states of consciousness include

- Sleep: stages include deep, light, REM
- Meditation, music, hypnosis
- Anesthesia
- Coma
- Pharmacological: marijuana, cocaine, LSD, opiates, alcohol
- Near-death experiences (NDEs)
- Physiological states caused by physical trauma to the brain; infections such as encephalitis, meningitis; O_2 deficiency
- Epilepsy
- Dissociation
- Spiritual experiences

As many experiencers have already discovered, consciousness is not simple. Many events take place that are not completely recalled. Were they asleep or awake, in a trance state, hypnotized, or under some form of mind control? Others seem only semi-real. Orbs, nonhuman entities, paranormal happenings such as ghosts and poltergeist phenomena, and travel, by the physical body, through solid surfaces, and perhaps through interdimensional portals, and out-of-body experiences have been commonly reported. Let's take a brief look at the latest research by physicists and scientists into the nature of consciousness.

According to the Dr. Edgar Mitchell Foundation for Research into Extraterrestrial and Extraordinary Encounters, the Quantum Hologram Theory of Consciousness (QHTC)

> suggests that we live in a multidimensional reality, and within this construct, humans are having contact with NHI in multiple formats, or "contact modalities" (e.g., UFO related contact and contact via Near Death Experiences [NDEs], Out of Body Experiences [OBEs], hallucinogenic substances, mystical meditation travel, channeling, remote viewing, sightings of spirits/ghosts and orbs, and other reported human encounters with NHI). The QHTC argues that all of these "contact modalities" are not separate phenomenon but instead are part of one interrelated phenomenon . . . a complex phenomenon that can potentially be explained by the physics of an all pervasive multi-dimensional Quantum Hologram.[3]

In our multidimensional universe, the concept of different planes of existence makes a lot of sense. With the densest plane being our life on Earth and all things physical, the next level is the astral, with the increasingly higher planes being those of the spiritual world. If consciousness exists continuously, throughout all planes and beings, that might explain the ease of interstellar/interdimensional travel for advanced beings, as well as all psychic phenomena.

The belief that consciousness is all pervasive, existing in all beings, organic and inorganic, is also shared by other modern physicists, parapsychologists, mystics, and shamans. In an excellent lecture, available free on YouTube, Bruce Greyson, MD, professor of psychiatry at the University of Virginia, discusses "Consciousness Independent of the Brain." He states that science cannot prove that thoughts originate in the brain and that consciousness can even exist without a functioning brain, citing cases of awareness reported after patients awaken from comas and anesthesia. They were able to describe events and conversations that took place when they were in a coma or under anesthesia.[4]

At the 2018 International UFO Congress, Caroline Cory's excellent film, *ET Contact: They Are Here,* won two awards for best and most popular film. It is available at no charge on Amazon Prime or can be rented or purchased.[5] This multifaceted film reviews current theories of quantum physics on the multiverse and consciousness, as well as descriptions of several NHI, and multiple reasons for their involvement with humanity. The film is uplifting and hopeful about our space community.

WHAT THE ERT HEARS FROM EXPERIENCERS

The following account of contact aboard a spacecraft was reported to our Experiencer Research Team. I include it because it illustrates the multilevel states of consciousness and also supports the theory of a holographic universe of multiple dimensions. Debra filled out our Experiencer Questionnaire and responded to my invitation for a call. In her initial email to me, she wrote the following:

> It happened about 22 years ago, but it was like it happened yesterday. I was pregnant with my daughter, I would say only a few months, when I went to take a nap. In the middle of my sleep, suddenly, my body was being sucked up into a tunnel as like a tornado, but with a very loud ear-piercing sound like a HUM. The sucked-up feeling was like a whirlwind. All I could do was call my son's name. I didn't know the reason for my calling him, but I knew I couldn't leave, I had to return to my son.
>
> The next thing I knew I was on a table covered in white sheets. It looked almost like a hospital room, which had

Nebulan Healers *(courtesy of Debra L.)*

stainless steel cabinets on the wall and the same stainless
steel table, which I was lying on. My body was covered and
my eyes were closed, yet I saw everything—even heard them
talking—but couldn't make out what was being said. I communicated with them telepathically, and all I could say was
"I have to go back. My son needs me. . . ."

There were several beings around my table on all sides.
They were wearing brown robes, but I could not see their
faces. They were wearing hoods. The robes had belts with
tassels on the ends. The sleeves were long as were their robes
with angel arms, almost like a bell bottom sleeve.

They were now communicating with me telepathically,
but I at this moment heard them in English. In the upper

left-hand corner, over my shoulder, was a being that was near a curtain, which was very long. He lifted his arm up and caught the curtain in a sweeping motion with his arm. As the being swept the curtain back, there was a light that was so intense I had to squint my eyes. The being then asked if I wanted to go to the light or come back. I yelled again, "I have to go back to my son! He needs me!" BOOM! I was back in my body so hard my whole body almost jumped off the bed.

I was terrified of what took place . . . so scared I made an appointment with a cardiologist to see if I'd had a heart attack or died. He took a few tests and told me no.

Since then I have awakened many times, thinking are they still coming for me? I don't have a clue. But almost nightly I think about that terrifying time, and hope it never happens again.

Coincidentally (or perhaps not coincidentally), I was the ERT member who received Debra's questionnaire and invited her to correspond. I also had an experience with a tall, brown-robed, and hooded "creature" when I was thirteen years old. I could not see its face, as the cowl of the robe covered its head. Looking back, I thought then that it was the Angel of Death or the Grim Reaper without a scythe. I remember having some sort of respiratory infection at the time. I screamed for my mother, and it disappeared. In 2016, I learned what "it" was, during a conversation with Cynthia Crawford, another experiencer who sculpted various extraterrestrials from around the universe. I had been looking for one for my Reiki room, and she directed me to her website. I looked at the artwork and was shocked to see a photo of the same robed being that I now know as a Nebulan Healer. The Nebulan Healers, according to her website, work with the Galactic Federation, protecting (certain) individuals to ensure their survival for roles in the future. (Though

Cynthia has since passed, her website is still active, and a colleague has continued to make the statues.)[6]

Without disclosing my own experience, I directed Debra to the website and asked if the Nebulan Healers resembled the beings she saw. Excitedly she agreed but said she was not ill when abducted. She then said that though she was not sick, her obstetrician had told her, after multiple tests, that her unborn child was diagnosed with Down syndrome and urged her to have an abortion. She refused. However, a few months after the abduction, her child was born without a disability! Originally terrified of the memory, she now feels blessed by the experience. This example illustrates again how important support, confirmation, and information are needed to normalize extraordinary experiences.

Why is this so important? I've described only one example of two individuals, the experiencer and the Experiencer Research Team member, separated by thousands of miles and several decades, sharing a healing experience by similar entities, both of whom were initially terrified by them for lack of understanding. What's interesting is that I have yet to encounter anyone else in my research or meetings who has had contact with this type of NHI entity. Coincidence?

Debra reported experiencing moving through walls, being transported through space, encountering strange and frightening creatures, talking to and understanding them telepathically, and being dumped back in bed!

It is no wonder that many experiencers are reluctant to talk with others, especially therapists who are not knowledgeable or do not believe these events are possible. On the ERT, we have spoken to many who were labeled as mentally ill by their family or therapists. Seeing, feeling, or hearing NHI entities, unfortunately, can easily be thought of as the hallucinations of mentally ill patients by untrained or closed-minded family or therapists.

In addition, many experiencers report continued telepathic and/ or visual communication from NHI entities. How do we distinguish what is real and what is imaginary? What is positive and what is harmful communication? These questions then lead many on a search for more information, new meaning, and confirmation. Continuing communication means continuing influence, but then how does this differ from other types of influence?

WHAT NOW?

What are your needs now? If you have gotten this far in this book, you may have already realized that sharing your story with someone knowledgeable and sympathetic is an important first step. Being believed without being judged is extremely affirming and reassuring.

Most experiencers who recall being on crafts with NHI entities describe telepathic communications, which are often experienced *after* their return. The difficulty then becomes: "Are these my thoughts or theirs? If they are communications, should I believe them and follow this 'advice' or these 'suggestions'?" I think using some common sense is important here! Is what you are getting helpful and loving? Do these thoughts make your life easier and more fruitful? If at any time they involve self-harm or harm to any other being or are negative in nature, you need to ignore or counter this communication!

Another suggestion is to write down information you think is received. If, for example, you are told that parking is available at a certain place, a person you meet is not trustworthy, or you should buy a lottery ticket, make a note if the information turns out to be true or not. Best of all, trust your gut!

I believe the old saying, "As above, so below." On our planet there is human conflict—within both individuals and nations and between loving, generous behaviors and greed and war. Why do we think that these conflicts are just on our planet? From the accounts of those who have experienced abductions, there are stories of pain, fear, indifference to suffering, as well as accounts of love, healing, and education. There are those NHI entities who care deeply about us and our planet, and those who are indifferent and selfish in their designs. As for intrusive thoughts/ideas, I believe we can judge them on this basis as well. If the thoughts are negative or unwelcome, I have found it useful to say, "No" and send back love! The spiritual growth that so many claim as a result of their contact demonstrates to me that the love we have been shown is a powerful weapon against the darkness of hate and greed.

EXPERIENCER GROUPS

Earlier, you learned about the benefits of attending an experiencer group. Unfortunately, such groups are not always available within reach of experiencers. Many UFO conferences have experiencer groups as part of their program. MUFON has a list of peer-facilitated support meetings for experiencers. When experiencers fill out the questionnaire on the MUFON website, they can, if they wish, be referred to the nearest support group and therapist. The ERT can refer them to an online support group if they do not live near one. The ERT member will have to contact the support group host and make the referral before the person is accepted.

INFLUENCE, MIND CONTROL, AND CULTS

Every day we are exposed to a constant stream of information from television, movies, our computers, and the Internet. Even the games we play on our tablets and phones have advertisements inserted, often to our annoyance. We are not immune to a vast, purposeful invasion of our senses designed to influence how we think, what we wear, what we buy, and how we vote. Every choice we make has been influenced at least in small part by the world around us. Next, let's look at influence and some simple tactics that inform our choices.

"I can admit it freely now. All my life I've been a patsy. For as long as I can recall, I've been an easy mark for the pitches of peddlers, fund-raisers, and operators of one sort or another," says Robert Cialdini, PhD, in the beginning of his book, *Influence: The Psychology of Persuasion.*[7] He identifies six social rules of conduct that we may barely be aware of; they make us susceptible to being unduly influenced by others, be they friends, marketers (TV, advertisements, news stories), the government, or even aliens. He calls these rules the "weapons of influence." Each of Cialdini's principles describes tendencies of human behavior that can be used to elicit compliance:

1. Reciprocation, or the act of give and take, creates a sense of obligation. This suggests that we should try to repay, in kind, what another has done or given to us. This repayment can be as simple as returning a favor, such as inviting friends who have previously fed us dinner. It is a common rule of polite society. This behavior can also be used to market items we might not really be interested in. An example is an invitation to a dinner at a fine restaurant where you know the provider will give a lecture on retirement communities, new home heating methods, or investment opportunities. (I must admit that early in our marriage my husband and I bought property at a ski resort in Vermont after being invited on a weekend trip, then selling it for a loss many years later! A sense of indebtedness—real, imagined, or manipulated—can be costly.)

2. Consistency in actions brings about commitment. Once you give (or give in), you'll give (or give in) again. This sets the stage for greater compliance. Saying no becomes more difficult, especially when your stance becomes public. Donate to

a charity or group, and you will forever be on their email or mailing list!

3. Understand the Rule of Authority: If an expert says it, it must be true. A classic example is a research project advertised at a college. Students signed up to participate in a study about memory. They were not told beforehand what was involved in the study but found that they were to give long, intense shocks to the students who got the answers wrong. No matter how the shocked students cried and pleaded to have the shocks stopped, they were denied. This was a famous experiment by psychologist Stanley Milgram.[8] The volunteers did not know that the people they "shocked" were actors and were not harmed. This experiment demonstrated that normal people can be psychologically manipulated into doing something they would otherwise never do by power of the authority invested in the teacher. You can substitute here other authority figures, such as government figures, doctors, or clergy.

4. Liking breeds friendship. Marketers, cult leaders, and groups make you feel wanted; in this way, you become part of something. There is a strong sense of belonging. Experiencers may be vulnerable because they are in a minority and may feel ridiculed and rejected by others.

5. Scarcity induces competition. You value what is rare, not easily available; its real worth is not necessarily an issue.

6. Consensus provides social validation or social proof. In general, people follow the lead of others, especially others similar to them.[9]

Why is understanding these rules of conduct important? Because those of us who have encountered abuse, trauma, or otherworldly events are more vulnerable to being taken advantage of by unscrupulous marketers, con artists, and even cults. The marketplace is full of those who would sell experiencers a variety of tools, classes,

INFLUENCE

1. Does the individual claim to be an expert or have a product that no one else has?
2. The more unusual the offer, the more evidence it needs.
3. Check it out! Google it, him, her, or the product/service.
4. What are the pros and cons, any niggling thoughts, or doubts? Honor these!

and experiences of the occult or contact phenomena. How can we differentiate what would be harmful and a waste of time and money from what could be beneficial or fun?

Mind Control

There is much history and mystery to the term *mind control*. It is now a rather negative and pejorative phrase. After the Korean War, the term *brainwashing* came into use to describe the harsh treatment of US prisoners of war that resulted in many of them renouncing the United States and American causes and beliefs. In 1961, Robert Jay Lifton wrote *Thought Reform and the Psychology of Totalism*.[10] This began the study of various types of persuasion that perhaps could explain how profound changes in thinking and behavior could occur in otherwise normal people. He also studied the behavior of the Nazi doctors and the operators of extermination camps, trying to understand how ordinary people could be led to do and believe in horrendous behaviors. Unfortunately, and to our shame, our own government has also experimented and researched mind control techniques on prisoners, government employees, and soldiers.[11]

Cults

Following the suicide of 918 members of the Peoples Temple, led by Jim Jones in Guyana in 1978, the subject of cults became of national interest. The UFO field is not without its cults as well, hence the importance of adding information about these groups here.

In 1997, thirty-nine members of Heaven's Gate dressed alike, took a mixture of phenobarbital and apple sauce, washed it down with vodka, and secured plastic bags around their heads to induce asphyxiation. This behavior was due to a belief in the coming destruction of the world and the necessity of salvation to "the next level," by boarding a spacecraft that was following behind Comet Hale-Bopp.[12]

Another large group, which one researcher defines as a new religious movement (NRM), has thousands of members, and among its prophet's teachings is that immortality is promised upon conversion to the group, and all others just die; they do not have a soul.[13] Is that a cult? Does it matter what we name a group or what the membership means to the individual?

HOW DO WE DEFINE *CULT*?

A cult is a group or movement exhibiting great or excessive devotion to a person, idea, or thing. According to the International Cultic Studies Association's executive director, psychologist Michael Langone, three characteristics, which may be present to a greater or lesser degree, help distinguish cults from other communities or groups:

1. Members are expected to be excessively zealous and unquestioning in their commitment to the identity and leadership of the group.

2. Members are manipulated and exploited, sometimes giving up families, careers, and education to work for the group.
3. Harm or threat of harm may come to members due to inadequate medical care or abuse (physical, psychological, or sexual).[14]

In addition, loss of the group may threaten their hopes for salvation, heavenly rewards, and eternity with their leader/God. Sexual activity may be defined as exclusive to members of the group or leader, or conversely celibacy or castration, as within the Heaven's Gate cult.

There is a great deal of difference between cults. Some, like the Peoples Temple and Heaven's Gate, are lethal, but most, thankfully, are less destructive. Groups range in size and the hold they have on an individual's life. Some have memberships of several thousand and are highly rigid, whereas others may have a relatively minor hold on a person's beliefs or lifestyle. Some cults have only a few members, yet cultic relationships have been described. They vary on their focus as well. Some may be religious; others Eastern or New Age, political, racist, terrorist, or psychological.

People do not knowingly join a cult or, for that matter, go to a psychic who will plunder their bank account. So, who joins a cult? Well, I did! Between 1977 and 1987 I believed that the psychotherapist I worked with was exceptionally brilliant and spiritually gifted. We shared a psychotherapy practice, or rather I thought it was shared, until he retired to another state, and I discovered a large theft of money and abuse of clients.

Brilliant, wealthy, and powerful people can be cult leaders, or also members and victims of cults. Let's explore the vulnerability that some experiencers may have to exploitative groups or individuals. These factors can include

- A desire to belong;
- Unassertiveness (an inability to say no or express criticism or doubt);
- Innocence or gullibility (an impaired capacity to question critically what one is told, observes, thinks, etc; questioning may be severely discouraged by the group);
- A need for absolute answers; impatience to obtain answers;
- Cultural disillusionment (alienation and dissatisfaction with the status quo);
- Naïve idealism;
- A desire for spiritual meaning and growth;
- Ignorance of how groups and/or marketers can manipulate individuals.[15]

Combine these factors with the appeal of a charismatic person and a product, service, or knowledge to market, and you have the possibility of exploitation. Max Weber classically defined charisma in 1922. He wrote, "Charisma is an exceptional quality in an individual who, through appearing to possess supernatural, providential, or extraordinary powers, succeeds in gathering disciples around him."[16] This description applies not only to cult leaders but also to some politicians, movie stars, and religious leaders. It is not necessarily a negative attribute of an individual. No doubt Gandhi, the Buddha, and Christ all had charisma and were able to attract followers to their teachings.

Protecting yourself in the marketplace of ideas, groups, services, and products requires some degree of discernment. Whether you are choosing which courses to take, which psychic to consult, or which UFO conference to go to, it is up to you to do some research. What are the pros and cons? *Who* endorses them? *Who* opposes or disdains them? Gather as much information as you can before your commitment. Are there any niggling thoughts or doubts? Are you rushing into it before you can change your mind? Perhaps the final test is, again, what your gut says about it.

GETTING PROFESSIONAL HELP

How do you know if you need professional help? When traumatic events happen, people respond differently in their ability to recover. Not everyone who is sexually assaulted, is in combat, or survives a tornado is permanently impaired. However, *all* will have some degree of immediate and acute traumatic symptoms. If these difficulties continue for months and years after the events, then professional help may be needed.

In previous chapters we discussed the importance of support groups, peer counseling, and the pros and cons of hypnosis to further recall amnestic periods and heal. However, if you are still experiencing distressful memories, you may have some or many of the symptoms of post-traumatic stress disorder (PTSD).

It has long been recognized that the results of war and combat produce hidden scars on the lives of soldiers. Since at least WWI, *combat fatigue, shell shock, combat stress,* and *war neurosis* have been used to describe what we now know as PTSD. But soldiers aren't the only ones who suffer the results of trauma. Victims of sexual assault, witnesses of overwhelming horror such as concentration camp survivors, and those who witnessed or were present during the Twin Towers attack in New York City and Washington, DC, on September 11, 2001, also may suffer. (As part of a small team of Veterans Administration psychotherapists, I participated in debriefings of VA personnel in New York City and New Jersey who witnessed the attacks from their office windows!)

It is not surprising that those involved with events involving nonhuman intelligences (NHI) may also suffer from PTSD. Some

WHEN IS PROFESSIONAL HELP NEEDED?

1. Do you have difficulty with controlling anger, depression, or sleep?
2. Do you have intrusive or upsetting memories, nightmares, or flashbacks?
3. Do you have overly negative thoughts about yourself and the world?
4. Do you have *any* suicidal ideation?
5. Unfortunately, not many therapists are familiar with contact experiences. Your therapist may choose to consult with an available mental health professional on the MUFON ERT.

NHI entities may resemble humans; however, many are quite different and may appear very frightening. Events on alien spacecraft may involve invasive physical procedures under what would understandably be frightening circumstances.

Nightmares, difficulty sleeping, intrusive thoughts, and reactivity to events that resemble the trauma accompanied by fear, anger, or just generalized anxiety and depression may be present. Guilt and shame may add to the distress. Many try to avoid anything that may resemble the trauma to avoid being triggered by fear. Due to the unique features of abductions/experiences with extraterrestrials, fear of ridicule—of being considered "crazy" or not being believed—add to the isolation of experiencers.

Many do not recall the entire event due to purposeful blocking of memories by NHI entities. The purpose of this blocking can only be surmised. The unreality of the experience(s) only adds to one's feelings of isolation and sometimes despair.

THERAPY

The good news is that PTSD is treatable. According to the American Psychiatric Association, the Department of Defense, and the

Department of Veterans Affairs, two treatments for PTSD are endorsed that I would recommend for experiencers. They are eye movement desensitization and reprocessing (EMDR) and cognitive processing therapy (CPT).

Before my retirement from the Veterans Administration in 2012, I utilized both EMDR and CPT with combat veterans and those with sexual trauma. In my private practice, I also used both therapies in the treatment of those who had left destructive cults. They are both "trauma-focused" psychotherapies. *Trauma-focused* means that the treatment focuses on the memory of the traumatic event(s) and its meaning to the client. These treatments use different techniques to help process the traumatic experience(s). They involve visualizing, talking, or thinking about the traumatic memory as well as changing unhelpful beliefs about the trauma.

Earlier in this chapter, you read about Debra's experience being taken on board a craft and encountering NHI entities who were frightening in appearance. Not understanding what was happening resulted in twenty-two years of nightmares and intrusive thoughts. Upon getting new information, Debra was able to reframe the entire episode, reduce fear, and develop gratitude toward the beings. Of course, this description is oversimplified, but this is an example of a cognitive change. Many of Debra's thoughts and feelings about the event were neutralized.

EMDR and CPT employ a mixture of cognitive work and desensitization of the trauma(s). Both are very important. It is not enough for those with PTSD to remember the event, but they also need to reduce or eliminate the powerful negative emotions that accompany those memories. EMDR actively targets the memories, intrusive thoughts, and nightmares for desensitization. Often, the client recalls more fully the event as well as the repressed memories. I can share an example of this from my work with a combat vet.

Joe served with a peace-keeping force in Bosnia in the late 1990s. I saw him for his PTSD a few years later, when he came to the Vet Center for treatment. His chief issue was that he shot a child, perhaps twelve years old, while holding off a crowd of villagers with his unit. The soldiers were ordered not to fire their weapons as the villagers angrily marched toward them. He didn't understand why he killed that child and was burdened with a huge amount of guilt and grief. While doing the desensitization of the incident using EMDR, he began by "seeing" the crowd advance. With bilateral movement of his eyes, which I guided, he suddenly stopped as he remembered the whole event. He recalled falling backward as the villagers advanced and his gun going off. Shocked and horrified by what happened, he recalled hearing his lieutenant yelling at him loudly and repeatedly, "Forget about it, forget about it." He did! Now that he recalled the situation, he understood that it was an *accident*. He did not deliberately kill that child. Still deeply regretful for the incident, he no longer believed himself to be bad or evil.

With CPT, much more emphasis is placed on the cognitive aspects of the trauma(s). This twelve-session scripted therapy has a manual and written assignments. It explores the meaning of the events and how they affect your sense of self, trust, and intimacy. The desensitization part is much simpler because two or more sessions are spent reviewing the client's written accounts of the trauma(s). This technique is not nearly as effective in desensitization and does not go into the actual trauma, but some prefer it to EMDR. (The bibliography provides information about finding these resources.)

We humans are hard-wired for self-preservation. Our senses are developed to protect us from danger, be it saber-toothed tigers or invading enemies. Many experiencers have had repeated abductions since early childhood. These abductions may have included physical and sexual abuse. Poking, prodding, performing surgeries,

SOME FOOD FOR THOUGHT

1. Feelings (emotions) arise from our thoughts and beliefs.
2. Primary feelings include anger, sadness, guilt, and joy.
3. Complex feelings such as rage, shame, despair, and elation result from adding strong beliefs about ourselves and the world.
4. *How* we *think* about something affects how we feel. Therefore, exploring and changing our beliefs will affect our emotions.
5. How we think and feel then affects our *behavior!*
6. Examining (and changing) how we think will alter how we feel and how we act.
7. If the thought, idea, or behavior doesn't feel right, change it! It doesn't matter what the source is.
8. Where do our thoughts come from if not from ourselves? Telepathy or undue influence (mind control)? Can we tell the difference? Does it matter?!

and extracting seminal fluids and ova—even if done with amnestic blocking by ETs—produce biochemical reactions within our bodies. Our nervous system is developed to enhance life preservation, and these kinds of traumas may cause significant changes in the nervous system.

During PTSD treatment, clients may experience times when trauma treatment alone does not seem to address these *sensory* reactions. Treatment for tactile defensiveness varies but usually includes education and insight into the cause of their disability and regular and daily exercises that assist in desensitization of issues such as touch, balance, and vibration. A common coexisting issue is, understandably, moderate to severe anxiety. There are controversies regarding the validity of the diagnosis as well as which treatment modalities are most effective. Because this is a more common diagnosis with children, research is directed at treatment of children, which will, in turn, benefit adult sufferers.

CONCLUSION

We are still in the beginning stages of helping those who have experienced contact with NHI entities. I believe that those who have had this experience will show the way, as their voices get heard and those who are just awakening to awareness of their contact come forward. Certainly, there is a great need for more support groups, educated therapists, and mostly, an educated public!

CHAPTER 8 QUESTIONNAIRE:
ARE YOU SUSCEPTIBLE TO CULT ABUSE?

Give yourself one point for each question you mark as true.

1. For much of my life I have felt like an outsider.
2. I am very uncomfortable when I don't know the answer to life's big questions.
3. People don't usually seek out my advice.
4. When I'm home alone, I like music or the television to keep me company.
5. I admit I have sometimes bought expensive things on an impulse.
6. I don't feel secure traveling to different cities alone.
7. Sometimes I am amazed by other people's insights and wisdom.
8. When I start a new school or new job, I try hard to make friends as quickly as possible.
9. Generally speaking, things are either right or wrong, or good or bad.
10. I would rather not rock the boat and challenge authority.
11. I worry about whether or not I am good enough to go to heaven.
12. I am too sociable to enjoy being alone.
13. It is possible to build an ideal community where everyone is happy.
14. I get very impatient when I don't know what to do about a problem.
15. One of the best things about regular church attendance is making new friends and socializing with the people there.
16. Spirituality is very important to me.
17. On occasion I have been betrayed when I should have seen the betrayal coming.
18. I have high ideals and most people don't live up to them.
19. When someone asks me for an inconvenient favor, I find it hard to say no.
20. I feel empowered and honored when I am part of a special religious ritual or ceremony.
21. Generally speaking, things in the world were much better years ago than they are now.

22. Occasionally, someone has convinced me to buy something, and later I realized I didn't like the item, or I paid too much for it.
23. I really want to feel part of something very special and noble.
24. Society would be much better if we all had the same beliefs.
25. I have been in long-term relationships, and after they end, I realize the person manipulated me many times.
26. Life was easier when a parent was telling me what to do.
27. Things in the world have never been as violent or as bad as they are now.
28. Confronting people is very hard for me to do, so I usually avoid it.
29. Sometimes I have done too much because I did not want to disappoint someone.
30. I don't mind when leaders get special treatment because they work hard and deserve it.

Scoring Chart

This questionnaire helps determine whether or not you may be susceptible to some form of cult abuse: the higher the score, the more susceptible you may be.

5–12 points: *You are an independent thinker with good critical thinking skills. You are not too easily influenced by others. You value diversity and are comfortable with ambiguity. You rarely seek approval from others and tend to live by your own values. You may have problems with authority. You are the least susceptible to a cult's influence.*

13–20 points: *You are very sociable and like to be part of a group, but you don't buy into everything the group believes. You know when you are being manipulated and may not allow it. You may not like confrontation, but you confront people when you have to. You are bothered for a long time when others disapprove of you. You may not be easily susceptible to a cult's influence, but sometimes people take advantage of you.*

21–25 points: *You don't feel complete if you are not part of a group, and you have a need to please others. You are flattered when you get attention and need some approval from others to feel complete. It is difficult to assert yourself, and you hate being alone. You may be more susceptible than average to a cult's influence.*

26–30 points: *You feel best when you are following a group and know what others expect of you. Approval from others is important to you, and you may change your opinion or behavior if others disapprove of you. You can be very loyal to a good leader. You may be more susceptible than most people to a cult's influence.*

Chapter 9

AM I BECOMING MORE PSYCHIC?

Ann Castle

One of the most remarkable and intriguing changes that a large majority of experiencers encounter is an increase in their psychic abilities and spirituality. About 65 percent of experiencers report increased psychic ability, visions, and spirituality; 80 percent report an increase in empathy; 45 percent report a physical healing; and 55 percent report a near-death experience.[1] There is not enough evidence yet to indicate what brain and consciousness changes initiated these experiences, but thousands of cases indicate links between NHI experiences and increased psychic abilities. This raises the question: are experiencers encountering NHI entities because they are more psychic than the general population, or are experiencers more psychic because of their encounters? Unfortunately, no one yet knows, so for now let's focus on the experiencers' association with various psychic phenomena.

BACKGROUND OF PSYCHIC ABILITIES AND SOCIETY

There is much evidence to support the theory that NHI and ET experiences follow familial lines and that genetic and biological manipulation by ETs may start in the womb. Therefore, experiencers may be different or "upgraded" from other humans. This difference may include increased psychic talent. For thousands of years there has been evidence that psychic ability runs in families and that it can be developed, so both of these factors may influence whether experiencers have more psychic talent than average humans.

For thousands of years societies have used trained shamans and psychics to predict events. Famous Greek oracles at Delphi served rulers for over 1,500 years, and they were respected throughout the world for their wisdom and accuracy, before a rise in Christianity's political power caused their downfall.

Unfortunately, for the past 2,000 years in the Western world, politicians and religious leaders have systematically punished people (especially women during the witch hunts) for developing their psychic abilities and convinced the majority of people that either these talents don't exist or that they are evil. Just as removing an eye from all newborn children would hinder those children's lives, repressing our natural psychic development has impaired the amount and quality of information that we can access to solve problems, develop intellectually or spiritually, and enrich our lives! This hindrance has allowed politicians and religious leaders to control societies more easily, and this repression continues today.

Consider this: would we be as easily controlled or fooled by others if we were all telepathic and instantly knew the thoughts, agendas, and feelings of others? There could be no betrayal or crime! Countless experiencers have indicated that ETs and NHI entities communicate with us and each other through telepathy. Plus, those who have experienced telepathy report that not just the idea is correctly communicated but also the context, conditions, exceptions, three-dimensional diagrams, emotions, and fine nuances of the idea are communicated in a blinding second! In other words, entire and complete communication of the idea takes place. This is far more complete communication than speech, which is thwarted by the limits of language and interpretation, and devoid of context, intent, and nuance.

Perhaps one day humans may communicate telepathically, which would greatly change society and relationships. I believe that ETs have been manipulating our gene pool since the first humans were on Earth and that we may have been telepathic in the distant past. I also suspect that the Bible story of the Tower of Babel indicates when ETs turned off our ability to communicate telepathically, forcing us to invent different languages, and causing communication chaos ever since.[2] Telepathy is such a powerful ability that telepathic humans would be difficult for anyone to control!

The famous psychic Ingo Swann, who worked for the US government as a psychic spy, wrote a book titled *Penetration: The Question of Extraterrestrial and Human Telepathy*. The book's central hypothesis is that if humans developed their psychic potential, especially telepathy, this would be an enormous threat not only to many social institutions but especially to Earth intelligence agencies and governments, who greatly fear losing control of the populace.[3]

Modern parapsychologists and psychics believe that psychic ability is another sense we are all born with, and the degree of talent depends on innate ability and training. So how does psychic ability work?

HOW PSYCHIC ABILITY OPERATES IN THE UNIVERSE

To understand how psychic ability works, it helps to have a basic understanding of the two kinds of physics that operate our universe: *mechanical physics* and *quantum physics*.

Mechanical Physics: Isaac Newton is considered the father of mechanical physics, which is the study of how *big things* like planets and objects operate: they are bound by laws of motion, thermo-dynamics, gravity, time, and space.

Through personal experience we learn that objects are separate from each other, they have no effect on each other at a distance, and they do not have consciousness. We experience that things are bound by linear time, space, gravity, and matter. We are told that things cannot go faster than the speed of light. I consider this the *old physics,* which is still valid in our three-dimensional world, but it coexists alongside the *new physics*—quantum physics.

Quantum Physics: Albert Einstein is considered the father of quantum physics, which is the study of how *very small things,* like subatomic particles, operate, which is very different from how *big things* operate. Subatomic particles have their own laws, can influence each other at vast distances, can "remember" actions and previous states, and *can carry information* in the form of light particles (photons) or waves. In addition, quantum physics strongly suggests that other dimensions exist, which may explain paranormal phenomena and some NHI encounters.

Quantum physics has shown us that there is a *relationship* between time, space, and gravity. This means that if given the technology (as ETs have), we could manipulate time, space, and gravity, and we could travel faster than the speed of light by bending space. We could also bend gravity around an object, causing light to bend around the object and rendering the object invisible. I think this may be why some UFOs often appear as blurry lights in the sky that pop in or out of sight because they are in the process of manipulating their gravitational fields.

Many experiments indicate that subatomic particles may also be self-aware, meaning that they have *some degree of consciousness* and this would mean that the universe itself is conscious! In addition, what human experimenters are thinking while they are conducting subatomic particle experiments can influence what the subatomic particles do! In other words, our thoughts interact with subatomic particles and support the increasingly popular belief that *our thoughts create our reality.*

Quantum Field: Quantum physics also gives us the notion of the quantum field, which can be thought of as an invisible cloud that connects all subatomic particles in the universe, meaning it exists inside and outside of us. Even our thoughts operate in this field, which creates the environment enabling psychic abilities, time travel, wormhole travel, ET travel, and NHI experiences. For experiencers who have had physical abductions, it is this field that ETs manipulate to create temporary holes in solid objects, allowing them to float people through walls and ceilings. It is also the quantum field that interacts directly with our body and mind, and enables us to obtain psychic information.

HOW PSYCHIC ABILITY OPERATES IN THE BODY AND MIND

Body: All living bodies have an aura. The aura is a biomagnetic energy field composed of photons of light and an electromagnetic field that surrounds our bodies like an egg. I was born with the ability to see auras, and I'm known as an *aura reader.* The body also has specialized energy centers called chakras, which serve as energetic portals through which energy is exchanged. It is through your aura and your chakras that you initially receive psychic information from the quantum field (more on this later). This information goes to the subconscious mind.

Subconscious Mind: One role of the subconscious mind is to communicate with the universe. It is extremely psychic and is the repository for psychic information. It receives quantum waves of information from the universe that connect all people and is the repository for psychic information. The subconscious mind remembers everything we have experienced. It remembers every hurt or every happy moment you've had and the *context* around these things. We know the subconscious mind remembers everything because a few people have been afflicted with a strange memory phenomenon called *hyperthymesia;* these people can remember every day of their lives. Also, hypnotic regression can help experiencers (or crime witnesses) retrieve memories.

The subconscious mind serves as a gatekeeper and filters what it allows the conscious mind to access at a given moment, so the conscious mind is not overwhelmed with irrelevant information. The subconscious does not understand time—everything exists in the present—just as time exists in the quantum field. The subconscious also holds the muscle memory of actions we perform while on "automatic pilot," such as driving or playing the piano.

One challenge is that the subconscious thinks in symbols, archetypes, and feelings, and may send us messages in code, such as sending us an image of a bell to represent a woman named Isabelle. In my experience this is probably the biggest obstacle psychics face, because in their conscious minds, they must interpret the subconscious symbols they receive and then wrap language around them to make them understandable. Once while working a major criminal case, I received a visual impression that the victim's body was "wrapped in blue." I misinterpreted this to mean she was wrapped in a blue blanket, when in fact she was in a blue barrel.

Our subconscious minds are like sponges, ready to absorb information from the quantum field, our environment, or the influences of others. It believes in *quantum physics*. This permeable quality of the subconscious helps us adapt and be more psychic, but it is also a double-edged sword that opens us to the danger of psychic manipulation.

Psychic Persuasion: Psychic persuasion is a form of mental manipulation or brainwashing that is perpetrated by ETs and governments. It causes victims to do things they would not ordinarily do. Since the subconscious is permeable to information, it is susceptible to external instructions. For example, ETs could psychically persuade a person who is ill in bed with a fever to suddenly drive thirty miles into the country in the middle of the night for an abduction. The person may be aware of driving and rationalize this behavior by thinking that the fresh air would be healing; after the event the person may realize this behavior is irrational.[4]

ETs can also implant *screen memories* into the subconscious to make you remember a different experience than what you had. Often screen memories dissipate over time so that you may suddenly realize what really happened. In my research I am surprised at the high number of experiencers who have phobias of clowns. Years later they realized that the childhood experience they thought they had with clowns was really with Grey ETs.

If you are in the presence of ETs and sense that they may be about to control your mind, you can thwart that attempt by confusing them. Often ETs urge us to look into their eyes, which allow them to initiate mind control. You should sing, rapidly change songs, dance a little, recite nursery rhymes, speak gibberish, and change thoughts and images every few seconds to confuse them. Never threaten the ETs. Sometimes if you appear crazy to them, they will not invade your mind.

There is a feedback loop between the subconscious and conscious minds, so new experiences from the conscious mind are stored in memory in the subconscious mind; and psychic impressions from the subconscious mind are sent to the conscious mind. Figuratively speaking, this two-way communication occurs in a portal, and the wider the portal, the more information flows. Also, the wider the portal, the more susceptible you are to paranormal experiences, which is why many experiencers have to deal with both NHI and the paranormal.

Meditation: *The single best thing you can do to develop any psychic ability is to meditate on a daily basis.* Meditation is the means to widen that portal, allowing more psychic information to come from the subconscious mind to the conscious mind. For centuries, adept yogis have considered psychic ability a mere by-product of meditation.[5]

Conscious Mind: The main role of the conscious mind is to solve problems, make decisions, and focus on the problem at hand. To focus well, we have become adept at ignoring some messages from the subconscious mind; plus, our society trivializes those messages, dreams, and hunches. These factors make psychic development challenging.

The conscious mind believes in *mechanical physics* and the limitations of time, space, and our three-dimensional existence. It wraps language around the impressions from the subconscious to categorize the experience and communicate it to others. Wrapping thoughts in a language always implies interpretation and judgment, which can misinterpret an intuitive message, just as I did with "wrapped in blue." It seems that the richer and more complex a culture's language is, the more logic, differentiation, meaning, and nuance can be packed into communication, but the less likely that culture is to understand or value intuition. The more simple a language is, the more likely that culture understands and values intuition. Some primitive tribes have a simple language, but they have shamans and psychic dreams, and they purposely nurture their intuition.

MAJOR TYPES OF PSYCHIC ABILITIES

Empaths: Almost all humans have some degree of empathy. From their own experiences, they can imagine how others feel in situations. However, empaths have a much stronger degree of empathy that is not necessarily based on their own experiences but is based on how well they are connected to the quantum field, what degree their subconscious absorbs the information, and how well their conscious minds can interpret it. *Once that portal between the subconscious and conscious mind is opened, psychic talents are easier to develop . . . and the more susceptible you are to the paranormal. Therefore, being empathic is the foundation for all other psychic ability.*

However, the worst part about being empathic is that you absorb emotions from others and may not be able to distinguish them from your own! You absorb both positive and negative emotions, but I focus on the negative emotions here because they are troublesome. Here are some characteristics of being empathic:

- You have a certain level of chronic anxiety and insomnia, which is not related to fear of NHI entities.
- You have chronic low-level depression. (I am not talking about clinical depression.) Try to notice where you are and whom you are with when you feel this depression the most. Is it at work, at home, or on the subway? Some buildings or rooms, such as courtrooms, hold terrible energy! Try to avoid those areas or people.
- Others say you are moody and you may be bipolar.
- You know when someone is lying to you or a loved one is in trouble.

- You have sudden thoughts or feelings that pop up out of nowhere.
- You can feel another's ailments and may know exactly on the body where the issue is.
- You overeat because subconsciously others have drained you of energy.
- When you leave a negative person or environment and are near a positive person, you suddenly feel better.

Clairvoyance: This broad term means clear seeing. It is a common psychic talent and conjures up stereotypes of carnival fortune tellers. Clairvoyance refers to visual images or premonitions of past, current, or future events. Clairvoyance also refers to *scrying,* which is the use of gazing upon a reflective surface (such as crystal balls or mirrors) and distorting your vision to obtain images. Remote viewing is a form of clairvoyance to view a distant target and is used by militaries, governments, and some private corporations. I remote-view for law enforcement. Sometimes clairvoyant images are triggered by touch (such as handshakes), photographs, dreams, or meditation.

Clairaudience: This term means clear hearing and refers to the ability of obtaining psychic information by sound, voices, words, or even music. Psychic information may come in the form of words suddenly coming to you or voices you hear. Tinnitus, or ringing in the ears (which is also a common trait among experiencers), may precede a clairaudient experience.

Clairsentience: This term means clear knowing and refers to the ability of obtaining psychic information through the energy centers in your body. You are usually not aware of this bodily process but suddenly you *just know something.* If you have ever correctly perceived someone staring at your back, distrusted someone you just met, or trusted your gut instinct, your clairsentience was at work. Everyone is at least slightly clairsentient. You may simply call clairsentience "my intuition" or "my gut feeling" while not realizing it is a psychic talent.

Clairsentience operates through our nervous system and is strongly connected to the nerves in our abdomens, as well as our chakras. Our solar plexus and our navels are both major chakras, which may be why our gut instinct can be so reliable. I believe clairsentience is connected to the neurological meridian lines used in Asian medicine and acupuncture.

Different people may have different sensations when their clairsentience is at work. You may get chills when you hear truth, headaches before a bad event, or flutters in your stomach when you know something. One FBI agent, immediately before apprehending a guilty suspect, gets the sensation of ant bites on the back of his neck: this tells him the suspect is guilty.

Aside from meditation, the best way to develop your clairsentience is to pay attention! When psychic impressions come to you, where in your body do you feel them? Learn to recognize the signs your body gives you when it is trying to communicate. This ability comes with awareness, time, and practice. One of the easiest ways is to learn to consult your gut. Drop your awareness to your gut when you are relaxed, upset, scared, and peaceful. Learn the differences! Do this in new situations or when meeting new people. What does your gut say about them? Usually, your first impression is correct. Habitually checking in with your gut several times a day will help you feel what your clairsentience is trying to tell you, which will make you more aware when your gut has information for you.

Psychometry: Some psychics that work with law enforcement pick up information from an object the victim handled; this is called psychometry, which is a form of clairsentience. Evidence suggests that we leave tiny bits of our DNA on everything we touch and that people talented in psychometry are sensitive to the DNA information.

Healing: This is the ability to influence the body's energy to alleviate pain, correct a malfunction, or speed up the natural healing process. You can learn to feel the energy in your hands and to direct it to injured or ill parts of a body for healing. All living beings have some ability to heal. The best healers psychically know where to lay their hands.

Dreams: Precognitive dreams are quite common, and almost all people have them. However, the problem with dreaming is that most of us don't recall our dreams. Dream recall can be enhanced by learning *lucid dreaming,* which is when people are aware they are dreaming and make a point of remembering them. Some psychologists believe that déjà vu (the feeling we have experienced the present moment before) is caused by our mind making connections between similar events so that they feel familiar to us, but many scientific experiments have proven that most déjà vu feelings happen because we previously dreamed the event and remember it when the event occurs.[6]

Although quantum physics, theoretical mathematics, and anecdotal evidence suggest that alternate dimensions exist, our technology is not yet capable of proving that alternate dimensions can be accessed via dreams. However, strong anecdotal evidence suggests that dreams may also access alternate dimensions, and more importantly, that NHI, ET, and paranormal experiences may also occur in alternate dimensions.

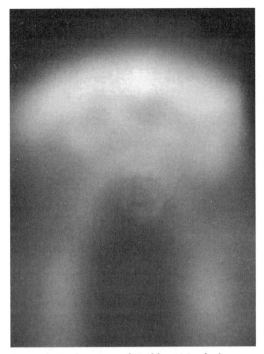

Aura photo *(courtesy of Kathleen Marden)*

Aura Reading: This is the ability to know information about people through seeing or sensing their physical aura. As mentioned earlier, the aura is a biomagnetic, electromagnetic energy field composed of photons of light that connects our bodies, spirits, and consciousness. It surrounds the body like an egg and has different layers with various colors and frequencies. The size and complexity of the aura depend on the species, age, health, and level of consciousness. The aura emanates in different colors from various energy chakras, with major chakras located in the head and torso. These chakras serve as energetic portals through which energy is given and received.

Since I was born with the ability to see the various colors and energy patterns in the aura, I can interpret a person's health, mental state, beliefs, attitudes, and other personal information with a great deal of accuracy.[7] This ability has proven helpful in uncovering the root causes of a person's problems or talents. It has also helped law enforcement by offering character analyses of suspects or deceased victims, and identifying who's who in hierarchies of gang members.[8]

With practice, most people can learn to sense the edges of the aura and to feel the presence of another even in a dark room. Practice sitting in a dark room alone and pretend you have mental feelers that emanate from your head out to the corners of the room. Push out your feelers around the furniture and walls. Ask your feelers if there are other entities in the room. Ask a friend to sit in a corner of the room and try to sense him or her. Learn how another entity feels in the space. With enough practice, you will be able to scan your entire environment rather quickly to see if there are any threats. Be patient because this talent may take months to develop well, but it is a handy method to knowing whether or not human or NHI intruders are around.

Aura Photography: Many people have paid to have their auras photographed. Unfortunately, unless the photograph is taken with a Kirlian camera—which is rare, very expensive, and usually found only in university laboratories—the photograph they received was *not* a photo of their aura! Fake aura photographs are taken with the person's hand on a metal plate, which measures the temperature of the hand that is superimposed over the person's photograph. A person with a cool hand will have a blue "aura," while a person with a hot hand will show a red "aura," and so forth. Changing the temperature of the same person's hand will result in differently colored "auras," just as mood rings changed colors in the 1970s. Besides, true human auras generally have four to six layered colors, not one.

Dowsing: This is the ability to use dowsing rods to find things, such as water or oil, or to use pendulums to determine *yes/no* answers to specific questions. Cave paintings in North Africa show that people have been dowsing for at least 8,000 years.[9] The snake-entwined caduceus was originally a dowsing rod.

There are two types of dowsing instruments: *dowsing rods* and *pendulums,* but they work on different principles. Dowsing rods are generally hazel wood, willow wood, or copper. They are used to find things, such as water, oil, minerals, metal, or old foundations. The rods move when they encounter differences in the electromagnetic field, which changes at the border of the ground and the sought-after object. For example, the electromagnetic field of the dirt will be different from that of the object. The dowser will use markers to indicate on the ground where the electromagnetic field changed, which outlines the location of the object. Sometimes the ground is not suitable for dowsing if there are underground pipes, caves, tunnels, electrical wires, or a very high water table because all these things give false readings and hinder dowsing.

Pendulums are more popular and easier to use. They are conical-shaped weights, usually of stone or metal, and attached to a small *metal* chain. The user rests an elbow on a table, holds the pendulum by the chain, waits for it to become very still, and asks a *yes* or *no* question. Eventually, the weight spins in either a clockwise direction for a *yes* response or a counterclockwise direction for a *no* response. Be sure you are not sitting over pipes, water, or wires that can give false readings.

Many famous people have used pendulums successfully, including Leonardo Da Vinci, Albert Einstein, Robert Boyle (the father of modern chemistry), Nazi General Erwin Rommel, and American General George Patton.[10] With practice, anyone can learn to get consistent and accurate results, which is helpful with decision-making. Modern science either debunks dowsing or claims not to know how it works. However, in my experience, I suspect pendulum dowsing works by accessing information from the subconscious, transmitting that information along the neurological meridians of the body, down the metal chain, and then very subtly—even invisibly—influencing the movement of the muscles to move the pendulum to indicate a specific answer.

Telekinesis: Usually, this refers to the ability to move objects with our minds. Although many people can do this occasionally, it is a very difficult skill to learn or control. Emotional intent is key to moving the object purposely; you must want to move the object very much. After concentrating on moving the object with great emotional intensity, suddenly stop thinking about it and the object may move. Usually, telekinesis is done by accident, when a person is upset or stressed, and random objects move without the person knowing he or she moved it. Sound waves can also be produced. This is the cause of poltergeist phenomenon mentioned in Chapter 6, and is most common in preteens, teenagers, and young adults, but in some people this phenomenon lasts a lifetime.

Telekinesis also refers to the ability to influence outcomes with our thoughts. I've known talented psychics who have been hired to use this talent in corporations to achieve specific agendas, which makes me suspect that some governments may also be using telekinesis to influence geopolitical outcomes.

Telepathy: This is the ability to read minds. It is more common than you think, and almost all of us remember instances when we have shared thoughts with a loved one, knew what someone was thinking, or expressed the exact same thought at the same time. This usually happens around people we are close to, which suggests that telepathy is more likely if we already have subconscious quantum connections to someone.

Telepathy involves both a *sender* and a *receiver* of information. Some people are better at one or the other, so pay attention to whether you are better at sending or receiving.

Many experiencers have related instances when ETs have initiated telepathy with them and made them telepathic as well, indicating we innately have this talent! As mentioned earlier, this form of communication sends the entire idea and all related information and context with it. Many reports of ETs indicate that they communicate among themselves with telepathy. When ETs are telepathic with us, we automatically (and unknowingly) wrap our own language around the telepathic thought because our conscious minds understand ideas best when expressed in our language. This is why ETs can communicate seemingly in any language, but they are not dealing with language at all—we are!

Many animal behaviorists and some scientists believe that animals use telepathy to communicate with themselves, other species, and humans. Animals think in images, not words. In my work as an animal communicator, I have found this to be true and have devised an easy way for you to communicate with your dog.

First, get your dog's attention and send a mental video of what you want him to do. Then drop the image. The dog will probably do the action because dogs love to please their humans. This exercise is helpful if your dog fears being abandoned when housed at a kennel. While dropping off your dog, send images of him passing a day and then a night. Repeat this for the number of days and nights he will be there. Send the final image of you coming back to retrieve him. This exercise works with cats as well because they are extremely psychic and connected to the quantum field, but they may choose not to do the action just because, well, they are cats. They may glance at you, acknowledging they received the message, and then look away, ignoring you.

Mediumship and Channeling: This is the ability to communicate with discarnate entities, usually the human dead, NHI entities, or ETs. This ability became most popular during the rise of the

Spiritualism religion in mainly English-speaking countries in the 19th century but lost popularity when many mediums were debunked. This talent differs from telepathy because the idea is communicated in the medium's language and/or in symbols, with all the difficulties of communicating with a language. Often the entity's personality is felt during communication, and flashes of symbols or visions are communicated as well.

There are slight differences between serving as a medium or a channeler. Mediums allow entities to communicate through them but retain control of the situation and communicate in their own voices. Channelers allow the entity to overtake their bodies and consciousness, and their voices and demeanor may change. Often channelers do not remember the channeling session. You should always say a prayer of protection before any mediumship or channeling session to help prevent negative entities from entering you.

Time Warping: This is not a usual psychic ability, but some experiencers have the ability to warp time and have experienced a speeding or slowing of time even when they are not near ETs, NHI entities, or paranormal events. The ability to warp time may be a by-product of encountering ETs or NHI entities, or of having achieved a certain level of psychic or spiritual development that can manipulate time. Although there are many anecdotal reports of this phenomenon, it is very hard to research because time warping is anecdotal, spontaneous, and difficult to reproduce.

Usually, time warping occurs when there is a very great need—a very strong intent—to be on time somewhere. The strength of the intent is key in precipitating this event. For example, I know two nursing students who regularly carpooled fifty miles each way over rough rural roads to attend nursing school at night. One evening when they had an important final examination to take, they had car trouble. The husband of one of the students managed to fix the car and witnessed the time they left. They somehow covered the distance in twenty minutes when it usually took them well over an hour.

CONCLUSION

Everyone is born with psychic ability, and experiencers seem to have extra ability. Experiencers often lead more complicated lives than most people because they are dealing with their own ET experiences, as well as other NHI or paranormal experiences, and misunderstood psychic experiences. They often have no one to confide in and feel as if they are living secret lives. Regardless of these challenges, increased psychic ability is a gift that can enrich your life and help you manage many situations. It may also be a precursor to a new, more evolved model of human that may be happier and more adept at managing our future.

CHAPTER 9 QUESTIONNAIRE: PSYCHIC TALENTS

If you have multiple psychic talents, this questionnaire is designed to help you determine your dominant talents. On paper, draw columns for the major psychic talents discussed. As you read the questionnaire, give yourself a point in each associated column for each true statement. The talent with the most points is your dominant psychic talent.

Empath:

1. Drama queens really drain me!
2. I have noticed when a group of people or a place depresses me.
3. I'm really moody, or I am easily moved to tears from poignant films or books.
4. Sometimes I strongly like or dislike someone for no logical reason.
5. I have had strong emotions pop up from nowhere.
6. I avoid being in large crowds because they tire me.

Clairvoyance:

1. I often say to people, "I see what you mean."
2. I learn best by watching demonstrations, and I never forget a face.
3. I often dream in full color and have a vivid imagination.
4. Sometimes visions (that are not my own) pop into my head.
5. I can sometimes see what loved ones are doing at a distance.
6. I like to draw, paint, or play with colors. Art and color are important to me.

Clairaudience:

1. I often say to people, "That sounds right!"
2. I am a great listener and have good musical ability.
3. Sometimes a voice in my head has stopped me from doing something dangerous.
4. I've heard loved ones calling my name from distant places when they were in crisis.

5. Sometimes I hear a tone or ringing in my ears before receiving psychic information.
6. I'm very sensitive to loud noises and can hear things at a distance that others miss.

Clairsentience:

1. I often say to people, "That feels right."
2. I learn best by doing something myself.
3. Sometimes I feel danger or butterflies in my stomach, or my bowels are upset.
4. Sometimes I just know things, and I don't know how I know them.
5. I'm a very good judge of character.
6. Sometimes I can feel an object a person owned and pick up a lot about that person.

Aura Reading:

1. Sometimes I see colors or flashes of light surrounding people.
2. I can tell what kind of mood people are in the moment they enter the room.
3. I have seen flashes of different-colored lights out of the corner of my eye.
4. I can guess someone's favorite color fairly easily.
5. Occasionally in public I feel someone so creepy I don't want to stand near that person.
6. Sometimes while lying in bed in dim light, I see a white layer over my arm.

Healing:

1. I know how to use my hands to help others heal.
2. I can feel energy flowing through my hands, and sometimes it is very hot.
3. I heal quickly from injuries.
4. People like to hug me.
5. Sometimes I look at people and know exactly where their bodies hurt.
6. People or pets love my massages!

Dreams:

1. I've had a few precognitive dreams or visions that have come true.
2. I often dream in full color and in great detail.
3. I can remember many of my dreams and have kept a dream journal.
4. I can sometimes direct my dreams or know when I am dreaming.
5. My dream life is important to me, and I look forward to dreaming.
6. I've visited with departed loved ones in my dreams.

Telekinesis:

1. Things often go "bump in the night" when I'm around.
2. Objects around me have moved on their own, especially when I was a teenager.
3. I have lived in a place that seemed haunted.
4. If I concentrate, I can move objects with my mind.
5. Sometimes I can make people change their minds by willing them to do so.
6. I'm a very physical person and good at sports.

Telepathy:

1. Many times I know what a loved one is thinking, or he or she knows what I am thinking.
2. Animals really like me, and my pets and I are well connected.
3. I often anticipate exactly what people are going to say.
4. My mental, inner world is very important to me.
5. I would rather read a good book than play sports.
6. I love learning new things.

Mediumship or Channeling:

1. My mind wanders a lot, and I often lose my train of thought.
2. I have sensed deceased loved ones in my presence.
3. I have communicated with deceased loved ones in my dreams.
4. I meditate (or can blank out my mind) easily or can be hypnotized easily.
5. I have no fear of opening my mind to another entity.
6. I have a strong desire to help people heal from their grief.

Chapter 10

WHEN YOU WANT IT TO STOP: COPING STRATEGIES AND RESISTANCE TECHNIQUES

Kathleen Marden

Have you ever made a survey of the descriptive terms used by the popular media when UFOs are the topic of discussion? You'll find words like *bone-chilling, horrifying, terrifying, screaming, horrendous, ghastly, dreadful,* and *terrible.* What message do you think is being embedded in the public's mind? It seems clear that we are being conditioned to experience fear and dread in association with UFOs and NHI contact. No written mainstream production or video mentions words such as *delightful, reassuring, encouraging, helpful, beneficial, heartwarming,* or *wonderful* when describing contact with NHI entities. We are being conditioned to expect the negative. One thing is clear: contact can be either positive, negative, or somewhere in between. Many experiencers believe that their contact events are beneficial. Others can find no value in continuing their experiences. How can you determine whether to continue your experiences or cut them loose?

Has your life become a living hell? Are you fearful of falling asleep? Is your sleep state dominated by highly negative entities who harm you or force you to engage in sexual relations against your will? Are you being taunted? Do you awaken with deep scratches in places that you can't reach? Are you being assaulted? If so, this chapter is for you. It will present a variety of resistance techniques that have worked for others, as well as sources for additional information.

Is abduction by nonhumans interfering with your sleep? Are you too tired during the day to carry out your employment responsibilities the way you would like to? Do you want the incisions, the scoop marks, and the bruises to end? Is your resistance to disease low because you are completely stressed out? Are you fearful of the night? Do you sleep with your lights and television on? Do you want to say goodbye to your hybrid children and the Grey masters who created them? Would you like to sever the cord that binds a Reptilian entity to you? If so, read on.

I wonder how many are reading this chapter first instead of last. In 2018, the Mutual UFO Network's Experiencer Research Team received requests for contact from 1,383 individuals who were seeking assistance. Many were seeking coping strategies or wanted their anomalous experiences to end. I was so concerned about this number of requests that I decided to search for ideas on how to end contact, how to end the victimization, and how to become strong and proactive. It is your human right to have control over your own body and mind. Anyone who denies you this is usurping your basic rights as a human being.

The United Nations has approved a "Universal Declaration of Human Rights." (Visit *www.youthforhumanrights.org* for the simplified version.) It lists thirty fundamental human rights. Here I have paraphrased the ones that apply to unwanted contact by nonhuman entities:

- We all have the right to life and to live in freedom and safety.
- No one has the right to hurt us or to torture us.

- No one has the right to detain us unfairly. If you are being detained by NHI entities, it is a violation of your human rights.
- You and your family have the right to privacy in your own home. No one has the right to enter your home uninvited or to intrude upon anything that belongs to you. This includes your right not to be monitored by NHI entities.
- We all have the right to our own thoughts. No one has the right to control your mind.
- We all have the right to our own beliefs, whether they are religious, political, or personal. Don't let anyone tell you that your negative experiences are truly positive or that your positive experiences are actually negative. You are capable of perceiving the nature of your own experiences. You decide.
- No one has the right to take away your human rights.

MY OWN STORY

Nearly three years ago, I made the difficult decision to engage in a secret experiment on the far edge of fringe topics. I agreed to attend meetings with a team of researchers who endeavored to explore the meaning of consciousness with a man who claimed to be in communication with a council of NHI entities. My healthy dose of scientific skepticism demanded credible evidence. This included a close encounter with a UFO and the manifestation of the NHI entities in the presence of our group. I received only a perfect circle of whirling water on my lake, as my body tingled with electricity, shimmering lights in my yard, glowing orbs moving along my lawn, and unusual lights in the sky. I hadn't anticipated the lessons we received on the nature of consciousness, physical dimensions, the history of our planet, and the council's concern over humanity's self-destructive behavior. I learned to communicate via telepathy and sensed the presence of these decidedly gentle, benevolent NHI entities.

I met Kevin Briggs, the channel for NHI consciousness, in September 2015, and several members of our group attended our first meeting in November that year. I trusted Kevin's credibility because he is a level-headed former police officer with a genuine interest in and curiosity about his newfound ability to engage in dual conscious physical communication. Our meetings ceased in September 2018, but a small group of us continue to meditate on a weekly basis. Kevin has written a book on his early life, *Spiritual Consciousness: A Personal Journey,* and is working on a new book of messages from the council to humanity.

I requested assistance from Kevin and the council after I was blindsided by evil in December 2018. I had made the decision to cease contact with experiencers of negative NHI entities because I am an empath and have experienced problems with negative entities. This was for my self-preservation. I thought that I was well protected, but something went wrong in December 2018, when I attempted to help an experiencer of contact with sadistic, evil entities. I let curiosity and compassion interfere with common sense and ended up with an oppressive dark cloud looming over me. This occurred despite my daily prayers, my strong religious beliefs, and the religious symbols in my home. This feeling was entirely uncharacteristic of me as I am normally a lighthearted, positive person. Somehow, I lost my connection with the benevolent council and began to spiral into a dark abyss. In desperation, I requested help from Kevin. He conferred with the council, and they agreed to help me. He hadn't told me this, when suddenly, I began to feel positive energy and the familiar tingling sensation that indicates my vibrational frequency is being elevated. (Theoretically, low vibrating negative entities cannot remain attached to higher frequency entities.) The council communicated several reassuring telepathic messages to me and darkness turned to light. They said, "You have been healed. You are revered. You are protected." Most of all I am thankful to Kevin and the benevolent council for their kindness. I am fortunate to have a connection with Kevin and the council. If I hadn't had them to call on, I would have had to seek outside help. Read on for suggestions that might work for you.

HOW CAN I BEGIN TO TAKE BACK CONTROL OF MY LIFE?

To take back control of your life, become proactive. Begin to undertake measures that will end the unwanted violation of your human rights. Do not let yourself believe this is impossible. Do not buy into the idea that NHI entities own you. You are an Earthling, and you have certain fundamental rights that must be respected and adhered to. The remainder of this chapter offers ideas on how to stop this violation of your fundamental human rights. I hope that at least one of these suggestions will work for you. However, I cannot guarantee that they will be successful. I can only state that others have achieved success when they undertook them.

Fear of the unknown is a ubiquitous condition among human beings. As children, we feared the dark, and some of us still walk with apprehension to the bathroom in the middle of the night. We fear what is unfamiliar to us, such as the traditions of other cultures and ethnic groups. We fear death and what will occur when we die. Trepidation in the face of the unknown is the most frequently mentioned cause of terror among experiencers. This is confirmed on MUFON's Experiencer Survey with the most prevalent trigger for terror in the night being fear of the unknown. The second and third most commonly cited causes of fear are loss of control and fear of being harmed.

Given these responses, would you feel more comfortable if you were advised of an upcoming visit in advance? Or would you lie awake feeling anxious and frightened? If you could learn a technique that would help you control your emotional response, would you? Would you practice self-hypnosis and do a rapid induction on yourself if it meant that you would remain calm and able to communicate with NHI entities? How would you feel if you were informed that the sweeping paralysis in your body is only a preparation and safety measure for the process of transferring you to an alien environment? What if you believed that they have no intention of harming you? What if they have healed you?

How would you feel if you were informed that you volunteered to save humanity before you were born? Many experiencers have recovered memories of coming to Earth as volunteers to help raise human awareness of consciousness and higher realities, to assist in humankind's evolution, and to save Earth from the destructive forces that have been controlling humanity. It might be worthwhile to explore your place on Earth and the reason behind your relationship with NHI entities before you make your final decision to end contact.

Are you a lifelong experiencer? If so, you might be a volunteer. Are you being harmed? If so, you have a good reason for ending contact. Will you miss your contact events if they cease? Will it feel as though you've left your family forever? Will you lose a major piece of who you are . . . your vital purpose in this lifetime? You might want to pursue therapeutic hypnosis before you make your final decision. You might be surprised by what you learn.

If you are certain that your contact experiences are unwanted and destructive, you must take several steps to prepare yourself for cessation. These steps will require strength of mind and purposeful action. You must prepare to behave assertively rather than aggressively. You might be required to project the emotion of love rather than hate toward your tormenters. Why? Negative entities feed off your human fear and loathing. There are several steps that you will have to carry out in preparation for their final departure.

PREPARE YOURSELF

If you have ever gone ghost hunting, played with a Ouija board, attempted to cast a magic spell, taken part in a séance, or channeled entities, you might have opened up a portal to yourself. If you have a relationship with a person who continuously drains your energy, you might be the recipient of that person's attachment. If you feel low on energy and your chakras are open to attack, you are a target for negative entity attachment. It is more common than you think. Some online sites will give you guidance on cleansing yourself and your home. Try their recommendations before you call in a professional. If you cannot clear the entity yourself, search for a specialist who can help you. This help will probably require a fee. You'll also need to find someone who can close any portals that are present. You can find a list of websites in Appendix A.

I have received requests for assistance from several people in the United States and in the Middle East who have reported the presence of tentacled entities. These are parasites from the astral plane that wrap their tentacles around your chakras and pull the energy from you. If they are present in your home, you'll notice an increase in your electric bill. They can also reach into family members to extract their energy. Seek assistance from individuals who specialize in negative energies detachment to have them removed.

I recently heard from a man who described his ET abductors as having the appearance of gargoyles. I had never received a report of this kind before. Online research at a site that assists people in negative entity removal said that they are from the dark side. These are demonic entities, not ETs.

Some researchers believe that ET energetic implants connect negative Reptilians to the humans they take advantage of. These implants make their victims readily accessible for contact and are responsible for the horrific nocturnal experiences that we hear

NHI entity in the doorway *(courtesy of Chad W., ERT)*

about in the popular media. Those who are taken night after night, raped, or forced to train for war have most likely been implanted with an entity attachment. These implants cannot be removed by a surgeon. They are energetic and must be removed by a specialist in energy work and negative entity removal. They are not easy to remove, but some specialists have been successful.

Reptilian attachment might have come to you in the disguise of a light being. But instead of experiencing positive energy and an increase in your vibrational frequency, you will feel neck pain, a headache, anxiety, anger, and heartburn. Spirit removal and karmic release techniques can remove Reptilian attachments. (I am not referring to the Reptilians of which some experiencers have a positive relationship.) See a specialist who has an excellent reputation in performing this work. Not all light workers can heal Reptilian attachments. Many have come under attack by Reptilians who are attempting to increase their hold on humanity. Positive ETs, angels, and Ascended Masters can assist in removing Reptilian energies. However, some people think that so-called Ascended Masters are negative Reptilians in disguise. This book's contributors and I cannot help you with this problem, but there are people who specialize in Reptilian attachment removal. See Appendix A for additional information.

First and foremost, ascertain that an organic medical condition, a psychiatric disorder, or a sleep disturbance is not at the root of your problem. Always seek your physician's advice. The most common question I receive from experiencers is, "How can I tell my doctor the truth? The doctor will think that I've gone crazy." You can talk to your doctor about the problems that occur whenever you fall asleep. You don't have to mention your suspicion that you are being abducted by NHI entities. You can say that your recurring nightmares are very frightening; over and over again, you dream of being captured by monsters and tortured. If that is the truth, it won't be perceived as a lie. If your symptoms began when you started a new medication, inform your doctor of its negative side effect. If you feel depressed, seek help from your doctor. Depression lowers vibrational frequency and can attract negative entities. If the problem occurs while you sleep, you might be referred for a sleep study to rule out a REM sleep disorder. And you might receive an order for a brain scan to rule out a tumor. At least you will rest assured that a serious medical issue has been ruled out.

Ensure that you are living in an uncorrupted body. Negative entities can easily attach to alcohol abusers. Fearful abductees who consume alcohol as a sleep aid are particularly vulnerable. Did you know that the word *alcohol* is derived from the Arabic word *al-kuhl*? It translates to body-eating spirit. Alcohol abuse lowers your body's vibrational frequency and opens you up to lower level negative entities. (You might want to read an interesting article on the spiritual effects of alcohol abuse at *thecostaricanews.com*)[1]

I know this to be true from a personal experience I had with a nice young man. He was a kind, loving person when we began our conversation. Later that evening he decided to have a nightcap that turned into three or four. It was then that I became the unwilling witness to a shocking transformation. Suddenly, his expression and demeanor changed. Our conversation stopped. There was an obvious change in his voice and appearance. He wanted to hug me, but he showed his teeth as if he intended to bite me. I called upon my Christian protector, Jesus, formed a cross with my fingers, and commanded the evil spirit to leave the young man's body. Immediately, his demeanor changed. He could not remember what had occurred a moment before. He was back in his body.

I am not directing you to call on Jesus. I would never attempt to impose a belief system on anyone. You have your own religious and spiritual beliefs, and you have the right to practice your religion accordingly. You might want to call on Allah, God, the One, or the highest intelligence if you find yourself in this situation. And if you are the person who is inviting spiritual attack through your abuse of alcohol, you might want to call on a higher power to assist you in ending the habit that is injuring you and those who love you. Alcoholics Anonymous is a good place to start if you cannot control your craving for alcohol.

The great challenge is to overcome the messages that have been imprinted on you by advertisers. We are barraged by images of beautiful, successful people consuming alcohol. The ads don't show you their behavior at the end of the night. How many have let their natural defenses down and engaged in inappropriate behavior? How many have acted out sexually? How many have acted out violently? How many have placed themselves in financial trouble? How many experience a feeling of shame when they remember their actions?

Why is the consumption of alcohol tied to spectator sports? Why do the parents of children who participate in sports gather together after the game and drink themselves silly in front of their innocent, malleable loved ones? It seems insane, but this behavior is promoted in some cultures and particularly in American culture.

When I was a child, companies with a commercial interest in the sale of alcohol inserted subtle messages into movies and not-so-subtle messages into advertising. My siblings and I watched a movie that depicted the wonderful effects of imbibing alcohol. The actors and actresses in the movie drank until they acted out in a silly manner. They laughed, fell down, got up again, and reveled in their intoxication. After watching their behavior, my siblings, cousins, and I whirled around and around until we became dizzy and fell to the ground. We could hardly wait until we could experience the wonderful effects of alcohol. The tobacco companies behaved in a similar way to convince America's youth that smoking was glamorous and beneficial. Who carries the responsibility for these messages?

Not long ago, heroin chic was a desirable fashion statement among advertisers of expensive garments. America now has a gigantic heroin abuse problem. In 2016, the small, fairly rural states of West Virginia and New Hampshire ranked numbers one and three in the United States for drug overdose deaths. Ohio was number two, and Pennsylvania and Kentucky ranked numbers four and five.[2] Nice children who were raised in good, loving homes are dying in large numbers. To make matters worse, there has been a move to classify addiction as a preexisting condition, so insurance companies won't have to fund treatment. America's children made a huge mistake. Are we to accept any responsibility for this? Or are we going to turn a blind eye to this silent massacre?

Authorities say that most heroin abusers began with prescription OxyContin. It was the source of the addiction, but when physicians were pressured into denying their patients prescription painkillers, the patients turned to the inexpensive alternative opioid—heroin. Like alcohol, it attracts negative entities, as does opioid use, whether or not it has been prescribed by a physician. I do not have firm data on this, but a disproportionate number of the abductees that I have attempted to help take OxyContin for back injuries. Their pain is unbearable, so they need something to maintain a tolerable level of existence. But I fear that negative interdimensional entities are feasting on their pain and suffering.

I have received a few letters from the mothers of war veterans who were seeking help for their sons who fought in the Middle East and now think they are being abducted by ETs. ETs do not insert themselves into the lives of humans over and over again on a nightly basis. Negative interdimensionals deserve the blame for these abductions. A different approach is needed. These people need help of a spiritual nature from those who are capable of removing negative entity attachments.

Did you know that idols, occult symbology, ancient relics, or your new antique collectible might be the root cause of your problem? The Egyptian god of death, Anubis, is a popular symbol among some collectors, but some say that it might attract negative energies. If you have a fixation on horror movies and occult memorabilia, and you are serious about bringing your problem to an end, remove them from your house. If you love them, rent a storage unit for a while. If ridding your house of these items doesn't help, you can try another suggestion. If your problem ends, you might wish to bring your decorations back one by one, to determine which one was causing your problem.

Often the souls of negative, deceased humans, who are afraid of moving on after death, choose to attach to an object they owned. Often these objects are wood, such as furniture, or mirrors. It is a good idea to sage any used furniture or other object you buy before bringing it inside. Be sensitive to how the room feels with the object in it, and if it feels oppressive or negative even after saging, get rid of the object! In addition, sometimes negative and depressing energy will not have consciousness associated with it but can literally give a room "bad vibes." Soft objects, such as upholstered furniture, carpeting, drapes, or old clothing can hold negative emotions and keep a room or house depressed for years after the negative person has left it. Sage and wash used clothing and hang it in sunlight before wearing it. Even long hair can retain the energy of the environment it was in while it was growing, but cutting off the hair solves the problem and gives the person an energetic makeover. Many people who have cared for negative, elderly family members have cured their depression after the person has passed on by cutting their hair, getting rid of the deceased's clothing, removing or professionally cleaning the soft objects in the room, and rearranging furniture or buying new furniture. Sunlight and fresh air are also excellent ways to improve the energy in a room.

The remainder of this chapter addresses two separate issues that are often cited as one nefarious all-encompassing phenomenon. Not all NHI entities are extraterrestrials. Some reside in Earth's astral plane and can masquerade as extraterrestrials. Some are negative and feast on human fear and negativity. There is a massive amount of evidence that extraterrestrials in highly advanced technological craft are active on our planet as well. The modus operandi between the two groups is distinct. One group torments the humans they attach to, and the other acts as scientists who focus on genetics, behavior, and their efforts to raise the human collective consciousness. One group rapes humans, leaves deep scratches on their bodies, and increases their victims' pain and negative behavior. The other can be frightening and interfere with the experiencers' emotional well-being, but knowledge can lead to understanding and perhaps acceptance. The ET groups claim that experiencers entered into a contract with them, to assist in human development, before they were born. Experiencers are split on their acceptance of this claim. Some accept it as true, whereas others believe it is false propaganda. If you do not buy into this claim, you might benefit from the following suggestions. If you are uncertain about the true nature of your contact experience, the information in this book will help you decide.

1. **Call upon a higher power.** This step is most important if you have a negative entity attachment, but it has been successful with all experiencers. If you are already participating in a religious faith and living it on a day-to-day basis, continue to do so. If you practice the rituals of your faith but do not live by the benevolent guidelines set down by your faith, change your thought patterns and behavior. This is of primary importance. Attending church and contributing money to charities will not help you unless you live by the guidelines of your faith. This applies to all religious faiths and is not limited to only one particular sect or belief system.

   If your heart is filled with hatred for an entire religious group, an entire race, or the inhabitants of an entire country, you are contributing to a negative collective consciousness. If your intolerance is fed by fear, you are contributing to the problem. Open your heart and bring love and healing to the human collective consciousness. Destroy the negativity.

Although the majority of experiencers become increasingly spiritual, as a by-product of their contact events, the experiencer survey indicated that 14.5 percent become less religious. This number increases to 17 percent among negative experiencers. When faith in a higher power is of primary importance for spiritual development, they turn away from it. If you find an NHI entity in your bedroom, call out in the name and authority of your deity or a higher power for protection. If you are an atheist and believe that science is the highest power, it will not prevent negative entity attachment. Seek out a specialist in the removal of attachments. This might be a minister, priest, shaman, light worker, or rainbow healer. (Denise Stoner offers additional information in Chapter 7.)

2. **Raise your consciousness.** Engage in consciousness-raising exercises. Our ET visitors do not share our collective consciousness. They vibrate at a higher frequency and are generally more spiritually inclined than the majority of Earthlings. They teach us that thought can impact humanity. It can create beauty or it can lead to great evil. Scientific experiments have demonstrated that loving thoughts can manifest to help a plant grow and flourish, and hateful thoughts can create disease and death in a plant. Cancer cells have failed to multiply when positive human thought came into play. It is extremely important for the survival of our species to raise humanity's collective consciousness. Doing so will lead to humanity's elevated vibrational frequency and an easier way of life for Earthlings. You can begin this movement through the practice of guided meditation. You'll find excellent consciousness-raising meditations on YouTube. They will not interfere with your religious beliefs. God is Love.

3. **Request protection.** Protect yourself before you fall asleep. Ask for protection from Buddha, Muhammad, Archangel Michael, Jesus, or whatever divine spirit protects you. Ask to be enveloped in pure white light and in rainbow healing light. Ask the Warriors of Light to protect you while you sleep.

4. **Be assertive.** If NHI entities enter your home, gather internal strength and confidence. Practice being fearless. Focus only on positive thoughts. Project love. Defy their attempts to create fear and negativity within you. This will take practice during your meditations. Remain silent but tell them telepathically to leave. They do not own you. They have no right to you. You have not given them permission to take you. It is your body, and no one else can enter it. No NHI has the right to attach to you.

5. **Sever your contract.** If you are being contacted and taken physically, and you have been informed that you had entered into a contract before you were born to assist in the development of humanity, you do not have to buy into this agreement. You do not have to continue doing something that makes you feel uncomfortable. You are not required to be locked into this contract. Break the contract. Tell them that you have decided that you do not want to continue in their program. You didn't know that it would have a negative impact on you and/or your family. It is frightening and unsettling. It is something that you no longer feel comfortable with, and you do not have to continue. Simply tell them that you want to end the contract. If they are benevolent beings who truly have human interest in mind, they will not force you to participate in a program that you no longer endorse or want.

From time to time I have appeared on Miesha Johnston's *Starseed Awakening* radio show. She is a hypnotherapist, host of two online support groups, and an experiencer. At a recent show, she, her cohosts, and I were engaged in a lively conversation when she brought up the topic of ending unwanted alien abductions. She informed us that experiencers have successfully ended contact by breaking their contracts. If the NHI entities are ETs and not interdimensional entities who have attached to your auric field for their own negative reasons, they will grant you a release from your contract. Miesha has a wealth of knowledge on this topic.

6. **Employ physical violence.** I am not an advocate for the use of physical violence against NHI entities. However, some resisters advise abductees to rise up and defend themselves just as they would if a human intruder had entered their private residence during the night. Spring up and grab your abductor by the neck. You might be able to harm him or her. Keep a weapon by your bedside to club, cut, or shoot the NHI entity. Be certain it is an unwanted intruder and not your spouse or child. If you engage in this form of violence against NHI entities, be prepared to be harmed. They protect themselves by taking control of you, and you might awaken with injuries.

7. **Use an LED flashlight.** Denise Stoner suggests this method for warding off NHI entities by shining an intense beam into their eyes. Purchase more than one intense, strobing LED flashlight and keep one under your pillow and another on your nightstand. You can store others in a handy, easily accessible place. When you become aware of NHI entities in your bedroom, shine the beam into their eyes and then turn on the strobe. They do not like this and will leave your room. Denise was successful in warding off a Reptilian intruder by using this method.

8. **Avoid eye contact.** Denise Stoner warns against looking into the NHI entities' eyes. They sometimes use an eye-to-eye communication technique to impart powerful messages.

These messages might be used for the purpose of controlling you. If you avoid eye contact, you might be able to reduce the power of the telepathic messages you are receiving. Close your eyes and focus on a positive memory that you can easily recall. Plan for this in advance, so you will be prepared. Or silently state, "I am full of love. Leave me alone."

9. **Using thought, create holographic images of yourself.** First, you will have to learn to meditate or enter into a deep state of relaxation. You'll find many relaxing meditations online. Select one or two that you enjoy. When you are deeply relaxed, in your mind create holographic images of your own body from head to toe. Use your mind to create thousands of these images of yourself. If family members are having problems with NHI interference, you can assist them by creating images of them with your mind. Theoretically, the mind can create these holographic image projections. When you have created enough of these images, the NHI entities will not be able to locate you. They will become confused and give up or relinquish their authority over you.

10. **Protect your family.** The most distressing situation for any parent is feeling helpless when their children are being harmed. One little girl confided to her mother that she felt frightened when the "sky people" took her to their house at night. She was too frightened to sleep in her own bed. Parents and family members can take certain steps to end generational abductions and generational attachments. This approach requires repeated telepathic communication directed at the perpetrators. Advise them to leave your family alone. Do not take your children; do not take your nieces and nephews; do not take your sister or brother; do not take your mother, your father, and so on. Make these statements assertively, not aggressively. Your success will depend on your ability to convey

a message that is not rooted in fear. Think or state, "Leave my family alone. You are not welcome here. We do not want to see you again." Be strong and rejecting, but remember not to show aggressive, threatening rage.

11. **Request help from family members.** This suggestion is closely tied to suggestion 10. It is founded in the idea that group resistance can achieve greater success than individual struggle. This approach is common in other cultures around the world where entity attachment is considered a fact of life. Extended families work together to overcome negative entity attachments and break the generational ties to undesirable contact. They work as a group to give emotional support to the afflicted family member and to overcome unwanted intrusions into the lives of their loved ones.

12. **Make a thought screen helmet.** This tinfoil hat idea might sound kooky to some readers, but one website makes the claim that it has only one reported failure since 1998. It requires the construction of a thought screen helmet lined with velostat, a packing material made of polymeric foil, impregnated with carbon black to make it electrically conductive. Its inventor, Michael Menkin, believes that it will scramble telepathic communication between aliens and humans. He states, "Aliens cannot immobilize people wearing thought screens, nor can they control their minds or communicate with them using their telepathy." (Visit *www.stopabductions.com* for additional information.)

Although I would love to assure you that one of the methods listed here will guarantee you success in ending your unwanted contact experiences, I cannot make this promise. I can only hope that you will find some relief from the various suggestions that might end your negative experiences. Know that I and the contributors to

Extraterrestrial Contact: What to Do When You've Been Abducted have dedicated our lives to helping others. We hope that we have been able to bring some comfort and relief to readers of this guide.

If you would like a formal investigation of your experiences, please file a report at *www.mufon.com.* If you wish to speak to a nonjudgmental listener on MUFON's Experiencer Research Team, please complete the thirty-question questionnaire in the ERT section of MUFON's website.

CHAPTER 10 CHECKLIST: ARE YOUR EXPERIENCES POSITIVE OR NEGATIVE?

Do you really want to end your experiences? Complete the following checklists by checking off all experiences that apply to you. Then tally your responses. If your experiences are primarily negative, you might want to take steps to end them. If your experiences are primarily positive, you might benefit from continuing them.

Are your experiences negative? _(Check all that apply.)_

☐ My experiences are terrifying.

☐ My experiences are disrupting my life.

☐ My sleep disturbances leave me feeling tired during the daytime.

☐ I have been fired from my job because I am too tired to work.

☐ I am taken on a very frequent basis.

☐ I am being forced to have sex with NHI entities.

☐ NHI entities treat me in a demeaning manner.

☐ NHI entities are evil.

☐ NHI entities are aggressive.

☐ NHI entities have harmed me or forced me to harm others.

Are your experiences positive? _(Check all that apply.)_

☐ I am sometimes frightened, but I can cope with my fear.

☐ My experiences are not too disruptive to my life.

☐ I am taken so infrequently that it doesn't have a big impact on my ability to sleep.

☐ My experiences have not had a major impact on my job.

☐ I am being treated in a business-like manner or better.

☐ I feel that I agreed to this before I was born.

☐ I feel that I am fulfilling a special purpose.

☐ I feel special because I am an experiencer.

☐ If my experiences ended, I would feel remorseful.

☐ I am part of a special community of experiencers with extraordinary gifts.

Chapter 11

GOING PUBLIC

Kathleen Marden

You have confirmed that your contact experiences are real. Your
bedside notebook is brimming with detailed memories of being
escorted to a hovering craft. You joined an online support group
and now realize that you are not alone. You are feeling a strong
desire to write a book, to share your experiences with others, to
appear on a television show. What now?

Your decision on whether or not to go public is the most important thing you will ever do. It might change your life dramatically
or leave only a tiny mark on ufological history. One thing is for
certain: once you step out from behind the curtain and perform in
front of an audience, you can never go back. Before you make this
life-altering decision, you have many things to consider.

It is important to discuss your plans with your family and friends.
How will they feel when you go public? Do they want you to use a
pseudonym? Will they disown you? Will they embrace you? How
will going public affect your employment? Will you be fired? Some
people have been. What kind of impact will this exposure have on
your children? Will it ruin their lives? And how will it affect you?
Can you take criticism without losing your self-esteem? Can you

hold your temper? Do you realize that there is very little money to be made by going public?

The days of widespread publicity for experiencers are over. Betty and Barney Hill, Travis Walton, Charlie Hickson, and Linda Cortile rose to fame because their experiences were unique.

The Hill abduction was the first of its kind to stir worldwide interest. It was investigated by scientists, some of whom believed it was real. There was substantial evidence to back up the Hills' statements. The Hills stood to lose more than they gained when they were thrust into the public eye in 1965, when a Boston newspaper reporter exposed their abduction as the result of a violation of confidentiality. This publicity brought prominent author John G. Fuller to them with a book proposal. They made the decision to cooperate with Fuller, and he carried their story to a wider audience in his book, *The Interrupted Journey* (1966). Fuller sold the story to *Look* magazine, which garnered additional publicity.

The fame the Hills achieved was overshadowed by a constant barrage of attacks on their credibility by skeptics such as Philip Klass, Dr. Donald Menzel, Dr. Carl Sagan, and a few less known but equally committed anti-UFO commentators and disinformants. Their home was entered unlawfully, and psychologically chilling operations were carried out. The harassment ramped up in 1969, after Barney's sudden death at age forty-six. Betty's tax records were taken and later strewn in a trail throughout her house. Her coats were removed from her closet and piled in a mound on her floor. Barney's scarf was draped over the top as an additional jab of distress to Betty. Her phone line was tapped, making it impossible for her to have a private conversation. The psychological campaign against Betty was so unnerving that I moved into her home to give her emotional support and to be another set of eyes. I became an eyewitness to a premeditated campaign that I believe was designed to push her over the edge. But Betty had excellent self-esteem, good judgment, and a fighting spirit. If the intent was to silence her, it failed.

Travis Walton did not make the decision to go public with his UFO abduction story. What propelled his story into the public eye was the fact that he had gone missing for five days and had witnesses who saw the UFO and reported the incident to the police. His trauma was magnified by the mistreatment he endured at the hands of disinformants such as Philip Klass. His character was smeared, and he was portrayed as a drug-crazed hoaxer. This barrage of maltreatment extended beyond Travis to his family and coworkers. (See my book with Stanton Friedman, *Fact, Fiction, and Flying Saucers,* for a detailed account of the conspiracy to debunk Walton's case.) As though he had not been traumatized sufficiently by his abduction aboard a disk-shaped craft of unearthly origin, by NHI entities, the go-to guys for the mainstream media were proficient at meting out additional pain. Their campaign involved malevolence of the worst kind.

Linda Cortile was thrust into the public eye by Budd Hopkins, the late UFO abduction researcher. Several people witnessed her abduction at 3:00 a.m. on November 30, 1989, from a window on the twelfth floor of her high-rise apartment near the Brooklyn Bridge. Twenty-three witnesses came forward to confirm seeing her being floated into a hovering craft. Yet, UFO investigators actively promoted their belief that it was an elaborate hoax based on a work of fiction she had read. She had insisted on maintaining her anonymity, but these investigators revealed her true name. Her life will never be the same, but she has done her best to maintain her privacy.

What do all of these UFO abductees have in common? Although they achieved notoriety, it was closer to infamy than distinction. A concerted effort was devoted to shaming all of them. The notion that extraordinary claims require exceptional evidence is promoted by skeptics. They demand a dead alien whose corpse can be examined by members of the National Academy of Science and declared nonhuman and not of this Earth. No amount of realistic physical evidence or multiple witness testimony will satisfy this demand. In other words, they insist on the impossible because the government would immediately cordon off public access to a UFO crash scene and confiscate the evidence.

THE CURRENT STATE OF AFFAIRS

Now that you've read the horror stories behind the public image, do you still want to go public with your story? Did you know that thousands, if not millions, of people around the world are having NHI entity contact experiences? This is no longer uncommon. Look around at the experiencers whose stories have appeared in the media in recent years. Denise Stoner's best evidence abduction in 1982 is featured in *The Alien Abduction Files* (Marden and Stoner, 2013). Her case is not as evidence based as the cases listed above, but there was substantial evidence of missing time after she and her husband saw a UFO. Two brightly lit craft descended on their vehicle and very suddenly moved them from four miles south of Jefferson, Colorado, to a new location on Trout Creek Pass, forty miles away, in what seemed like a moment. They had amnesia for the events that occurred over a two- to three-hour period. It had been daylight, and now it was very dark. People were awaiting their arrival at a predetermined time, but they failed to show up. There was great concern over their temporary disappearance. It was not the first, nor would it be the last abduction Denise experienced.

When Denise decided to go public, we anticipated that she would come under scrutiny and condemnation just like others have in the past. However, something seems to have changed. She faced little criticism. Her story was portrayed accurately on television by the Travel Channel and received a positive response. There was a difference, and it was for the better. Could this response be attributable to the manner in which Denise carries herself? She is not an attention seeker. Her persona is that of an intelligent, mature, well-spoken woman. She holds important positions in MUFON and has a track record as a highly respected investigator. There is little to criticize in Denise.

Others have not been treated with the respect that Denise has. Flamboyant self-proclaimed experiencers have a tendency to draw criticism from skeptics. You will find them creating a stir on Facebook and other social media sites. Their lives are in constant turmoil, and they sometimes claim to be under government surveillance. They post a flurry of photographs of themselves in various poses and outfits. It appears that they are in competition for the biggest story and the most friends on social media. They tend to be indiscriminate when they select social media friends, so they draw bullies and trolls to themselves. The criticism that is heaped on them creates another whirlwind of outcries garnering sympathy from their loyal supporters but leaves their lives in turmoil. Their lives become a vicious cycle of endless upheaval and resolution. It is not a good path to follow.

MEDIA APPEARANCES

If you have the opportunity to appear on television, ask questions before you agree to be filmed. Find out how your story will be treated. What channel will it be carried on? What can the filmmakers offer you as compensation for your time? Know that they will have their own agenda, and you will not have editing rights. They are producing a show that will appeal to the widest audience possible. Their goal is to make as much money as possible on their show and to build a name for themselves. Be careful; not all of them are honest.

You will be asked to sign a media release granting the production company permission to use your real name, your image, your statements, your recordings, and exclusive rights in all media and territories in perpetuity to exploit your story worldwide and forever. Read the contract fully and carefully before you sign it. Some of the sleazier production companies will request the right to slander or defame you. Never agree to this clause. You deserve respect. Be certain that you will not be made into a laughing stock. If you carry yourself professionally and well, you should be fine. Credibility is the key.

One production company contacted me to request a copyright release for segments of the Hills' hypnosis sessions with Dr. Simon. They wanted the few excerpts in which Betty and Barney were most terrified. This request made me feel extremely uncomfortable because the production company clearly planned to paint a horrendous image of the Hills' abduction experience. Although the abduction was frightening, the NHI entities they encountered offered reassurance that they did not intend to harm the Hills. The nonhuman entities showed compassion. They imparted the message that they had to complete a few simple tests, and when they had accomplished this, the Hills would be released unscathed. Betty's NHI escort apologized for frightening her. They were not monsters.

Barney had only one powerful emotional reaction, and Betty had two. I objected to this production company's plan to falsely portray the Hills' events and refused to cooperate with them. Dr. Simon's heirs decided not to release any of the Hills' hypnosis recordings because they are personal medical records.

On another occasion, a production company contacted me for assistance in locating experiencers who were willing to be interviewed for a television production. As the conversation developed, the person on the other end of the line advised me that he was seeking the most eccentric experiencers I could recommend. When I asked why he wanted eccentric people, he informed me that bizarre people appealed most to the public's entertainment desires. Do you think that I recommended anyone? Absolutely not! I was outraged! Experiencers are not fodder for comic entertainment! No honest person should be subjected to ridicule and disrespect! This is a highly sensitive subject that should be managed with accuracy, compassion, and understanding.

WRITING A BOOK

Perhaps you have documented years of contact experiences and you want to write a book to help others understand what contact entails. You might have passed through the several stages that Ann described in Chapter 4. You have moved from shock and denial through fear and anger. You've explored your experiences through hypnosis or might have had EMDR therapy. You've felt the isolation of not being able to tell anyone—of holding your secret inside. It hasn't been easy, but you have flourished and recalibrated to a new and awesome understanding of what contact means. It is so important for others to know this is for the greater good that you want to risk it all and spread the word. How should you begin?

Educate yourself. The Internet is brimming with companies that will publish your book for a price. They have employees who will read your manuscript at a cost and offer to edit it for a fee. They will then charge you to publish your book, and you'll have the opportunity to purchase copies of it for private sales. But who will buy it? Who will market it? How will you publicize it? Who will you employ to design your cover? If experiencers have never heard of you, will they purchase your book? If someone pirates your work, will you hire a lawyer? There are a multitude of possibilities to think about before you take this big step.

You'll have to decide whether to pay for print copies or to work out a contract with Amazon to sell your book online as an eBook. Amazon has an on-demand application called CreateSpace that you might consider. You can find it at *www.createspace.com*. You also can find a directory for self-publishing at *www.writersdigest.com*. These sites do not list all of the companies that might offer to publish your book for a price, so you should widen your search. Look for self-published UFO books, and you'll find companies that cater to this niche market. David Carnoy has an article on self-publishing at *www.cnet.com*. It elucidates for you the important things you need to know before you make the decision to self-publish.

Finding a reputable professional publisher is another matter. Few books are ever published by a professional publishing company. Publishers are seeking proposals from accomplished writers who have a track record. They do not charge their authors for the production of a book. The author generally has an agent who submits the proposal to the publisher and negotiates an advance and the terms of a contract. There are deadlines to meet, and the book must adhere to the topics outlined in the proposal. A word count is agreed upon in advance and must be adhered to. The author must submit a list of media appearances and the names of famous persons who will write endorsements to promote the book.

The publisher reserves the right to design the book cover and title the book. The publisher employs a legal team, a macro editor, line editors, and artists. The publisher's employees will secure the copyright and ensure that the book meets certain legal standards. All photos that are not the sole property of the author must be accompanied by signed releases. There must be footnotes and a bibliography. Generally, the book must be written in good journalistic style and must be as close to perfect as possible when it is submitted to the publisher.

The publisher employs a publicist to assist with the book's promotion, and the sales department promotes the book to booksellers. It might be marketed in hard cover, soft cover, eBook, and audio book formats. The author agrees to promote the book through radio shows and appearances that have been arranged by the publicist. The book might be marketed to foreign countries and published in foreign languages. From these efforts, the author receives royalties on the sale of the book and reserves the right to purchase books for sale on their website and at public appearances and conferences. The process is different from self-publishing. It is my personal choice because I am a researcher, author, and public speaker, not an accomplished businessperson, lawyer, or publicist.

In closing, I wish to express my gratitude to you for purchasing this book. I hope that you have benefitted from it. I attempted to cover a wide range of concerns that experiencers have expressed to me. Because I do not have expertise in all of the areas that contact encompasses, I invited three of my colleagues on MUFON's Experiencer Research Team to share their knowledge with you. I am grateful for their contributions.

Thank you very much!

Kathleen Marden
MUFON Director of Experiencer Research

Appendix A: Suggested Websites

Most serious researchers consider the following websites to be authentic and mostly trustworthy. This list is not inclusive of many fine ufologists or websites but is meant to be a starting place for you. It can be difficult for even excellent researchers to always know or publish the absolute truth, so it is best to read their information, compare it to other information, and keep an open mind.

UFOS AND ET CONTACT

- Kathleen Marden, a UFO and contact researcher, author, and niece of Betty and Barney Hill, *www.kathleen-marden.com/*.
- The Mutual UFO Network: Home of MUFON's Experiencer Research Team, *www.mufon.com*. Link to the ERT at *www.mufon.com/experiencer-research-team.html*.
- National UFO Reporting Center, one of the oldest sites for UFO reports, *www.nuforc.org/*.
- *Journal of Abnormal Abduction Research (JAAR)* is an excellent journal on abduction research and experiences. New issues are not being produced, but the older journals have valuable information on the experiencer enigma. JAAR is sponsored by the UFO Research Center of Pennsylvania, led by Butch Wittkowski, *http://uforcop.com*.

- UFO Sightings Daily, an interesting site with unverified UFO reports, photos, and videos, *www.ufosightingsdaily.com/*.
- UFO Research Center of Pennsylvania, a good comprehensive site on investigated UFOs, cryptozoology, and the paranormal, *http://uforcop.com/*.
- A consciousness-oriented website, the Dr. Edgar Mitchell Foundation for Research Into Extraterrestrial and Extraordinary Encounters (FREE), *www.experiencer.org/*.
- A good site on historical abductions, but some advertising to click through, *https://ufocasebook.com*.
- International Center for Abduction Research, Dr. David Jacobs's site, *www.ufoabduction.com*.
- Dr. John Mack, a Harvard psychiatrist, author, and early researcher of the experiencer phenomenon, *http://johnemack institute.org/*.
- Derrel Sims, a ufologist and author specializing in implants, *www.alienhunter.org/*.
- Linda Moulton Howe, a ufologist, journalist, and author who also investigates high strangeness, *www.earthfiles.com/*.
- Alien Jigsaw has an abundance of articles and information on ET contact, *http://alienjigsaw.com/*.

ENTITY ATTACHMENTS AND ALIEN ABDUCTION RESISTANCE

- Steve Deeks D'Silva and Lauren D'Silva, "Entity Removal: Clearing Entities and Astral Wildlife from People and Places," *http://www.entity-removal.co.uk/default.html*.
- Dr. Lawrence Wilson, "Soul Attachment and Release," *https://drlwilson.com/Articles/POSSESSION.htm*.
- Spiritual Science Research Foundation, *https://www.spiritual researchfoundation.org/spiritual-living/health-effects-of-food*

-*and-drinks/spiritual-side-effects-of-alcohol-drinking/*. Watch the interesting video of an experiment conducted by the SSRF.

- Texas Ghost and Spirit Intervention, "Spirit Attachment and Possession Symptoms," *www.texasghostandspirit.com /parasitic-entities/entity-and-spirit-attachment-and-possession -and-symptoms/*.
- Dr. Rita Louise, "Attached Entities: The Bad Guys of the Spirit World," *https://soulhealer.com/attached-entities-bad-guys -spirit-world/*.
- Jessica Dao, "Understanding and Clearing Difficult Negative Energies: Reptilians," *http://thepyramidoflight.com*.
- Joseph Jordan and Guy Malone (Christian resisters), *www.alienresistance.org*.
- Michael Menkin's thought screen helmet, *www.stopabductions .com*.

PSYCHOLOGICAL/SPIRITUAL RESOURCES

- EMDR International Association, *www.emdria.org/*.
- Cognitive Processing Therapy, *https://cptforptsd.com*.
- Quantum Healing Hypnosis Practitioners, *www.dolorescannon .com*.
- International Cultic Studies Association, *www.icsahome.com*.
- Do an Internet search for the spiritual effects of alcohol abuse. There are several interesting websites such as: *www .spiritualresearchfoundation.org*. Watch the video of an experiment conducted by the Spiritual Science Research Foundation.

Appendix B: Suggested Reading

We have listed our favorite books below. It is sometimes difficult to select books because some are reliable and others are not. We stand by the books listed here. They contain trustworthy information. Keep in mind that this is not a complete list of books on the topic of contact with NHI entities.

ALIEN ABDUCTION/ET CONTACT

- *Captured! The Betty and Barney Hill UFO Experience* by Stanton Friedman and Kathleen Marden
- *The Alien Abduction Files* by Kathleen Marden and Denise Stoner
- *The Dual Soul Connection* by Suzy Hansen
- *The Forgotten Promise* by Sherry Wilde
- *Fire in the Sky* by Travis Walton
- *Intruders* by Budd Hopkins
- *Witnessed* by Budd Hopkins
- *The Allagash Abductions* by Raymond Fowler
- *The Andreasson Legacy* by Raymond Fowler
- *Communion* by Whitley Strieber
- *Dimensions* by Jacques Vallee
- *Encounter at Buff Ledge* by Walter Webb
- *Abduction* by John Mack
- *Coronado* by Yvonne Smith

- *How to Defend Yourself Against Alien Abduction* by Ann Druffel
- *Captured Souls* by Ann Castle
- *Beyond UFOs: The Science of Consciousness and Contact with Non Human Intelligence. Vol. 1* by The Edgar Mitchell Foundation for Research into Extraterrestrial and Extraordinary Experiences

EXTRADIMENSIONAL CONTACT

- *The Extra Dimensionals* by John DeSouza

CLEANSING AND HEALING

- *Remarkable Healings* by Shakuntala Modi, MD
- *Unquiet Death* by Dr. Edith Fiore
- *Spirit Release: A Practical Handbook* by Sue Allen

CULTS

- *Take Back Your Life* by Janja Lalich and Madeleine Tobias
- *Influence: The Psychology of Persuasion* by Robert Cialdini

Notes

INTRODUCTION

1. Ann Druffel is also the author of *Firestorm* (Columbus, NC: Wild Flower Press, 2003), the biography of Dr. James McDonald, a highly respected scientist whose career was placed in jeopardy when a disinformant with malice in his heart sought to destroy him.

CHAPTER 3

1. Dr. Bernice Andrews. Originally found at a daily news website that is no longer available.

2. For additional information on hypnosis, see Kathleen Marden, "A Primer on Hypnosis," *www.kathleen-marden.com.*

CHAPTER 5

1. Ted Davis, Don C. Donderi, and Budd Hopkins, "The UFO Abduction Syndrome," *Journal of Scientific Exploration* 27 (2013): 22.

2. Kenneth Ring and Christopher Rosing, "The Omega Project: A Psychological Survey of Persons Reporting Abductions and Other UFO Encounters," *Journal of UFO Studies* 2 (1990): 89.

3. Susan Blackmore, "Abductions by Aliens or Sleep Paralysis?" *Skeptical Inquirer* 22, no. 3, May/June 1998, *www.csicop.org.*

CHAPTER 6

1. *American Heritage Dictionary,* Second College Edition, (1982), s.v. "paranormal."

CHAPTER 8

1. Wikipedia, s.v. "Sense," last modified on January 23, 2019, 20:08, *https://en.wikipedia.org/wiki/Sense.*
2. *Merriam-Webster,* s.v. "consciousness (*n.*)," accessed January 26, 2019, *www.merriam-webster.com.*
3. The Dr. Edgar Mitchell Foundation for Research into Extraterrestrial and Extraordinary Encounters (FREE), *www.experiencer.org.*
4. Bruce Greyson, "Consciousness Independent of the Brain," YouTube video, 1:24:18. *www.youtube.com.*
5. Caroline Cory, dir., *ET Contact: They Are Here* (Tallahassee, FL: OMnium Media, 2017). Available free on Amazon Prime, as well as for rent or purchase.
6. Cynthia Crawford, "Sculptures Page 5," *www.etsculptors.com.*
7. Robert B. Cialdini, *Influence: The Psychology of Persuasion* (New York: Harper Collins, 2007), xi.
8. Wikipedia, s.v. *Obedience to Authority: An Experimental View,* last modified on September 23, 2018, 04:41, *https://en.wikipedia.org/wiki/Obedience_to_Authority:_An_Experimental_View.* See also Stanley Milgram, *Obedience to Authority: An Experimental View,* reprint ed. (New York: Harper Perennial Modern Thought, 2009).
9. Madeleine Tobias and Janja Lalich, *Captive Hearts/Captive Minds* (Alameda, CA: Hunter House, 1994).
10. Robert Jay Lifton, *Thought Reform and the Psychology of Totalism* (New York: W. W. Norton, 1961).
11. Harvey M. Weinstein, *Psychiatry and the CIA: Victims of Mind Control* (Washington, DC: American Psychiatric Press, Inc., 1990).
12. Benjamin E. Zeller, *Heaven's Gate: America's UFO Religion* (New York: New York University Press, 1994).
13. Susan Palmer, "When Contactees Found 'Cults' . . . The Case of Raël and Prophets of UFO Religions" (lecture, International UFO Congress, Fountain Hills, AZ, 2018).

14. Tobias, Madeleine, and Janja Lalich. *Captive Hearts/Captive Minds*. (Alameda, CA: Hunter House, 1994).

15. Janja Lalich and Madeleine Tobias, *Take Back Your Life,* 2nd ed. (Berkeley, CA: Bay Tree Publishing, 2006).

16. Irvine Schiffer, *Charisma* (New York: Free Press, 1973), 3.

CHAPTER 9

1. Kathleen Marden, "The MUFON Experiencer Survey: What It Tells Us About Contact and the Implications for Humanity's Future," *MUFON 2018 International Symposium Proceedings*, Irvine, CA, July 2018.

2. Genesis 11:1–9 (King James), *www.kingjamesbibleonline.org.*

3. Ingo Swann, *Penetration: The Question of Extraterrestrial and Human Telepathy* (Rapid City, SD: Ingo Swann Books, 1998), xi.

4. Stephen Bass, "Psychic Persuasion: Exploring a New Concept," *Journal of Abnormal Abduction Research*, UFO Research Center of Pennsylvania, March 2014, *http://uforcop.com/assets/jaar-march-2014.pdf.*

5. Swami Panchadasi, *Course of Advanced Lessons in Clairvoyance and Occult Powers* (Whitefish, MT: Kessinger Publishing, 1916).

6. Ian A. Wilson, "Theory of Precognitive Dreams," *www.youare dreaming.org.*

7. Ann Castle, "Aura Facts and Questions," *www.aurareadings.com.*

8. Ann Castle, "For Law Enforcement," *www.anncastle.net.*

9. Lloyd Youngblood, The American Society of Dowsers, Inc., *https://dowsers.org/dowsing-history/.*

10. Barb Feick, Ohio Buckeye Dowsers, *barbfeick.com.*

CHAPTER 10

1. "The Spiritual Consequences of Alcohol," *Costa Rica News*, March 27, 2017, *thecostaricanews.com.*

2. "Which States Have the Biggest Drug Problems? Here Are the Rankings," *Pennsylvania Real Time News*, May 26, 2017, *www.pennlive.com.*

Selected Bibliography

Alien Resistance. *www.alienresistance.org.*

American Heritage Dictionary, Second College Edition. Boston: Houghton Mifflin Company, 1982.

Blackmore, Susan. "Abductions by Aliens or Sleep Paralysis?" *Skeptical Inquirer* 22, no. 3. May/June 1998.

Cannon, Julia. "Dolores's Career Biography." *www.dolorescannon.com /about.*

_____. "What Is Quantum Healing Hypnosis Technique?" *www .dolorescannon.com.*

Cialdini, Robert. *Influence: The Psychology of Persuasion.* New York: Harper Collins, 2007.

Clancy, Susan A., et al. "Psychophysical Responding During Script-Driven Imagery in People Reporting Abduction by Space Aliens." *American Psychological Society* 15, no. 7 (2004): 493–97.

_____. *Abducted: How People Come to Believe They Were Abducted by Aliens.* Cambridge: Harvard University Press, 2005.

_____"Memory Distortion in People Reporting Abduction by Aliens." *Journal of Abnormal Psychology* 3, no. 3 (2002): 455–61.

Cognitive Processing Therapy. *https://cptforptsd.com.*

Cory, Caroline. *ET Contact: They Are Here.* Tallahassee, FL: OMnium Media, 2017.

Costa Rica News staff writers. "The Spiritual Consequences of Alcohol." *Costa Rica News.* March 27, 2017. *thecostaricanews.com.*

Crawford, Cynthia. "Sculptures Page 5." *www.etsculptors.com.*

Dao, Jessica. "Understanding and Clearing Difficult Negative Energies: Reptilians." July 2015. *thepyramidoflight.com.*

Davis, Ted, Don Donderi, and Budd Hopkins. "UFO Abduction Syndrome." *Journal of Scientific Exploration* 27, no. 1 (2013): 21–38.

D'Silva, Steve Deeks, and Lauren D'Silva. "Entity Removal: Clearing Entities and Astral Wildlife from People and Places." 2010. *www.entity-removal.co.uk.*

Dr. Edgar Mitchell Foundation for Research Into Extraterrestrial and Extraordinary Encounters. *www.experiencer.org.*

EMDR International Association. *www.emdria.org.*

Friedman, Stanton, and Kathleen Marden. *Captured! The Betty and Barney Hill UFO Experience* (Franklin Lakes, NJ: New Page Books, 2007).

_____. *Science Was Wrong* (Pompton Plains, NJ: New Page Books, 2010).

_____. *Fact, Fiction, and Flying Saucers* (Pompton Plains, NJ: New Page Books, 2016).

Greyson, Bruce. "Consciousness Independent of the Brain." YouTube video, 1:24:18. *www.youtube.com.*

International Cultic Studies Association. *www.icsahome.com.*

Lalich, Janja, and Madeleine Tobias. *Take Back Your Life.* Berkeley, CA: Bay Tree Publishing, 2006.

LeLieuvre, Robert, Lester Velez, and Michael Freeman. "Omega 3: Revelation or Revolution: A Comparative Study of Abductees/Experiencers and Community Comparison Control Participants." April 2010, *http://theedgeofreality.proboards.com.*

Lifton, Robert Jay. *Thought Reform and the Psychology of Totalism.* New York: W. W. Norton, 1961.

Louise, Rita. "Attached Entities: The Bad Guys of the Spirit World." *soulhealer.com.*

Mack, John, Budd Hopkins, David M. Jacobs, and Ron Westrum. "Unusual Personal Experiences: An Analysis of Data from Three National Surveys Conducted by the Roper Organization." Las Vegas, NV: Bigelow Holding Corporation, 1992.

Marden, Kathleen, "The MUFON Experiencer Survey: What It Tells Us About Contact and the Implications for Humanity's Future," *MUFON 2018 International Symposium Proceedings,* Irvine, CA, July 2018.

Marden, Kathleen, and Denise Stoner. *The Alien Abduction Files.* Pompton Plains, NJ: New Page Books, 2013.

Martin, Malachi. *Hostage to the Devil.* San Francisco: Harper, 1992.

Menkin, Michael. "Thought Screen Helmet." *www.stopabductions.com.*

Merriam-Webster. *www.merriam-webster.com/dictionary/.*

Mutual UFO Network Experiencer Research Team. *www.mufon.com.*

Palmer, Susan. "When Contactees Found 'Cults' . . . The Case of Raël and Prophets of UFO Religions." Lecture, International UFO Congress, Fountain Hills, AZ, 2018.

Parnell, June O., and R. Leo Sprinkle. "Personality Characteristics of Persons Who Claim UFO Experiences." *Journal of UFO Studies* 2 (1990): 45–58.

Pianin, Eric. "The 10 Worst States for the Deadly Drug Crisis." *Fiscal Times.* May 15, 2017. *www.thefiscaltimes.com.*

Ring, Kenneth, and Christopher Rosing. "The Omega Project: A Psychological Survey of Persons Reporting Abductions and Other UFO Encounters." *Journal of UFO Studies* 2 (1990): 59–98.

Rodeghier, Mark, Jeff Goodpastor, and Sandra Blatterbaur. "Psychosocial Characteristics of Abductees: Results from the CUFOS Abduction Project." *Journal of UFO Studies* 3 (1991): 59–90.

Saunders, David R., and R. Roger Harkins. *UFOs? Yes! Where the Condon Committee Went Wrong.* New York: Signet, 1968.

Schiffer, Irvine. *Charisma.* New York: Free Press, 1973.

Spanos, Nicholas, Patricia Cross, Kirby Dickson, and Susan DuBreuil. "Close Encounters: An Examination of UFO Experiences." *Journal of Abnormal Psychology* 102 (1993): 624–32.

Texas Ghost and Spirit Intervention. "Spirit Attachment and Possession Symptoms." *www.texasghostandspirit.com.*

Tobias, Madeleine, and Janja Lalich. *Captive Hearts/Captive Minds.* Alameda, CA: Hunter House, 1994.

US Department of Veterans Affairs. "PTSD and DSM-5." *www.ptsd.va.gov.*

Warren, Donald I. "Status Inconsistency Theory and Flying Saucer Sightings." *Science* 70, no. 3958 (1970): 599–603.

Weinstein, Harvey M. *Psychiatry and the CIA: Victims of Mind Control.* Washington, DC: American Psychiatric Press, Inc., 1990.

"Which States Have the Biggest Drug Problems? Here Are the Rankings." *Pennsylvania Real Time News.* May 26, 2017. *www.pennlive.com.*

Wikipedia. s.v. *Obedience to Authority: An Experimental View.* Last modified on September 23, 2018, 04:41. *https://en.wikipedia.org/wiki/Obedience_to_Authority:_An_Experimental_View.*

Wilson, Lawrence. "Soul Attachment and Release." December 2017. *www.drlwilson.com.*

Youth for Human Rights International. "Universal Declaration of Human Rights." *www.youthforhumanrights.org.*

Zeller, Benjamin E. *Heaven's Gate: America's UFO Religion.* New York: New York University Press, 1994.

About the Author

Kathleen Marden is a leading researcher of contact with non-human intelligence and an author and lecturer. She is the director of experiencer research for the Mutual UFO Network and an advisory board member and consultant to the research subcommittee for the Dr. Edgar Mitchell Foundation for Research into Extraterrestrial and Extraordinary Encounters. Marden is the author of several books, including *Captured! The Betty and Barney Hill UFO Experience* and *The Alien Abduction Files*.

To Our Readers

MUFON BOOKS

The mission of MUFON BOOKS, an imprint of Red Wheel Weiser, is to publish reasoned and credible thought by recognized authorities; authorities who specialize in exploring the outer limits of the universe and the possibilities of life beyond our planet.

ABOUT MUFON

The Mutual UFO Network (*www.MUFON.com*) was formed by concerned scientists and academic researchers in 1969 for the specific purpose of applying scientific methods to the serious study of UFO sightings and reported human/alien interactions. MUFON's mission is "The Scientific Study of UFOs for the Benefit of Humanity" with the intent to unveil and disclose credible information free of distortion, censorship, and lies, and prepare the public for possible implications.

ABOUT RED WHEEL/WEISER

Red Wheel/Weiser (*www.redwheelweiser.com*) specializes in "Books to Live By" for seekers, believers, and practitioners. We publish in the areas of lifestyle, body/mind/spirit, and alternative thought across our imprints, including Conari Press, Weiser Books, and Career Press.